DATE DUE

AP 20 '0?			

DEMCO 38-296

FROM IDEA
TO FUNDED PROJECT

GRANT PROPOSALS
THAT WORK

BY JANE C. BELCHER
AND JULIA M. JACOBSEN

ORYX PRESS
1992

The rare Arabian Oryx is believed to have inspired the myth of the unicorn. This desert antelope became virtually extinct in the early 1960s. At that time several groups of international conservationists arranged to have 9 animals sent to the Phoenix Zoo to be the nucleus of a captive breeding herd. Today the Oryx population is over 400, and nearly 800 have been returned to reserves in the Middle East.

Copyright © 1973, 1992 by Jane C. Belcher and Julia M. Jacobsen

Published by The Oryx Press
4041 North Central at Indian School Road
Phoenix, Arizona 85012-3397

Published simultaneously in Canada

Printed and Bound in the United States of America

∞ The paper used in this publication meets the minimum requirements of American National Standard for Information Science—Permanence of Paper for Printed Library Materials, ANSI Z39.48, 1984.

Library of Congress Cataloging-in-Publication Data

Belcher, Jane C. (Jane Colburn), 1910–1991
    From idea to funded project : grant proposals that work / by Jane
C. Belcher and Julia M. Jacobsen.
     p. cm.
    Rev. ed. of : A process for development of ideas. Washington :
Government Relations Office, c1976.
    Includes bibliographical references and index.
    ISBN 0-89774-710-0
    1. Endowments—United States—Handbooks, manuals, etc.
2. Education—United States—Finance—Handbooks, manuals, etc.
I. Jacobsen, Julia M.   II. Belcher, Jane C. (Jane Colburn), 1910–1991
. Process for development of ideas.   III. Title.
LB2336.B43 1992   91-41706
370'.79—dc20   CIP

Contents

Preface   v

Acknowledgments   v

PART I: A PROCESS FOR DEVELOPMENT OF IDEAS   1

Introduction   3
  Purpose   3
  Institutions and Ideas   3
  A Cooperative Approach to Developing Ideas   4
  Who Needs this Guide?   4

Origin and Early Development of an Idea   6
  Role and Responsibility of the Institution   6
  How to Develop an Idea   6
  Role and Responsibilities of the Originator of an Idea   7
  Specific People and Their Tasks   7
      Originator of the Idea/Project Director   7
      Department Chair   8
      Department Members   8
      Academic Dean   8
      Chief Fiscal Officer   8
      President/Chancellor   8
      Grants/Sponsored Programs Officer   8
  The System of Development Begins to Operate   9

The Proposal: A Design for Putting an Idea to Work   12
  What Is in a Sound Proposal?   12
      General Considerations   12
      The Specific Parts of a Proposal   13
          Cover Sheet   13
          Table of Contents   13
          Abstract   13
          Problem Statement   14
          Goals and Objectives   15
          Procedures   15
          Evaluation   16
          Dissemination   18
          Facilities   18
          Personnel   18
          Budget   19
          Appendix   21
  Tests for Soundness of a Proposal   21
      General   21
      Review Process Criteria   22

Finding a Source of Support   30

Submission of a Proposal   32
  Cover Sheet   32
  Letters of Endorsement   32

     Letter of Transmittal   33
     Typing Requirements   33
     Finally and First: Follow Instructions, Follow Instructions   34
     The Final Check   34

Grant Administration   35
     Communication from and with the Sponsor   35
     Preparation for Securing and Expending the Grant Funds   35
     Negotiation and Acceptance   36
     Rejection/Self-Appraisal/Resubmission   37
     A Case Study for Administration of a Grant   37
          Anyville College Receives an Award   37
          The Cast of People Involved   38
          First Actions to Be Taken   38
          Spending the Grant Funds   38
          Anyville College—Post-Award Policy   38

Evaluation   49
     Importance of Evaluation to the Sponsor   49
     An Agency Requirement for Evaluation   49
     Preparing an Effective Evaluation Plan   50
     An Example Evaluation   50
          Evaluation of "Central Virginia Tomorrow" (CVT)   50

Conclusion   63

PART II: BASIC RESOURCES   65

Section I.   Acronyms   67

Section II.   Essential Basic Information Sources   69
     A. Publications   69
     B. News Releases   69
     C. Telephone Books   69
     D. Government Printing Office (GPO) List of Publications   70

Section III.   Other Sources of Assistance and Training   71
     A. Partial List of Education Organizations   71
     B. Other Washington Metropolitan Area Addresses   72

Section IV.   Forms and Required Information   73
     A. Classifications of Types of Grant Applications   74
     B. Department of Defense (DOD)   74
     C. Department of Education (ED)   80
     D. Department of Health and Human Services (HHS)   82
     E. National Endowment for the Arts (NEA)   86
     F. National Endowment for the Humanities (NEH)   97
     G. National Science Foundation (NSF)   104
     H. U.S. Department of Agriculture (USDA)   108
     I. Other required forms and necessary information   111
          1. Examples of Application Forms and Guidelines from Two Private Foundations   111
          2. A format for a *Curriculum Vitae*   116
          3. Acknowledgment Card   117
          4. Certification and Assurance Forms and Regulations   118
          5. Sample Drug-Free Workplace Policy Statement   128
          6. An IRS Letter of Determination   129

Section V.   Annotated Bibliography   130

Index   135

Preface

Ideas are products of individual human minds. Some of the ideas that emerge in educational and comparable institutions are potentially as important to the institutions as their endowments, and it is these ideas that are the concern of this guidebook: how to encourage their articulation, how to muster the cooperation necessary to turn them into formal blueprints, and how to secure whatever support is needed to see them materialize as projects serving the interests of the originators and their institutions.

Today's Christopher Columbus must find a different kind of patron, usually a foundation or government agency known to have an interest in the area of the quest. Once a possible sponsor has been selected, a proposal must be written, a proposal so well prepared and so convincing that it will receive serious consideration for support in competition with other proposals. This guidebook will assist you in conducting your search for a sponsor, in writing a proposal, and in all the preliminaries leading to these two acts, including developing the idea into a detailed outline, securing support of those who will be affected by the project, and conducting research for appropriate funding sources.

This new and expanded edition of IDEAS, now titled *From Idea to Funded Project: Grant Proposals that Work, Fourth Edition*, contains listings of useful resources and the most recent data on forms and required information for submission of proposals. This fourth edition reflects changes in the names of agencies and in regulations governing grants to nonprofit organizations. Because of the increased emphasis that grant-making agencies place on accountability and evaluation of funded projects, we have added new sections on the administration of grants and the evaluation of projects.

All names and addresses of agencies and organizations and all required documents included in this book were current in 1991. Our advice throughout the text is to double-check with the appropriate agency to be certain you are aware of the most current requirements.

Acknowledgments

The authors wish to express appreciation to Phyliss Reddington of the Association of College and University Offices, Inc. in Washington, D.C.; Robert L. Chase, Sweet Briar College; Richard Rossi and Allen Sinisgalli, Princeton University; and the many program officers and foundation officials who contributed ideas to this and earlier editions of this book. A special note of thanks must go to Barbara Belcher Mericle and John L. Jacobsen for proofing and objective editing.

PART I: A PROCESS FOR DEVELOPMENT OF IDEAS

Introduction

PURPOSE

This book discusses how institutions, and the individuals who make up those institutions, create and develop ideas. Though reference may be made more frequently to institutions than to individuals, the reader must never forget that it is the people who count, and it is the ideas they produce that are the heartbeats of the institutions. The people within an institution can be classified as either those who actually perform the institution's primary function and those who play a supporting role, the administrators. The partnership between these two groups can and must create an atmosphere that eliminates whatever reluctance people feel in expressing ideas and stimulates the germination of ideas. Although in general it is the role of the administrative staff to welcome the ideas produced by members of the institution and assure moral, institutional, and financial support for those worth adopting, those roles are often reversed; that is, an individual in either position may at one time be a creator and at another time a supporter of developing ideas. In spite of shifting roles, the ideal partnership maintained in a healthy institution guarantees the production and nurturing of ideas. This book provides suggestions that will help maintain this partnership.

Ideas range over a spectrum from good to bad, and this year's bad idea may become next year's good idea. How can ideas be selected, put into motion, doctored, trimmed, embellished, fitted to other ideas, and attuned with institutional goals? How can they be judged feasible, in terms of resources both within and outside the institution?

The life of an idea, from the moment of its emergence to the time of fruition, particularly when it needs help from outside the organization, can be long and often hazardous. The object of this guidebook is to provide a pattern or method for directing an idea through its entire existence. We, leaning on our own and others' experience, believe this method is adaptable to varied institutions, varied demands within the institution, and varied species of developing ideas—from those within a small department to those affecting the entire organization, from those involving purchase of equipment to those involving radical alterations in the tasks of many people. This pattern ensures the continuous involvement of all individuals who will be affected by the idea or who can influence its development, and provides a continuous, step-by-step evaluative process. By minimizing or eliminating hazards through constant evaluation, the pattern will lead to a mature, refined proposal and a significant and successful project.

The purpose of this book will have been achieved if it aids educational and other institutions in ensuring ferment of ideas and then turning those ideas into realities by finding and applying the needed human, material, and financial resources.

INSTITUTIONS AND IDEAS

Any organization is the fruit of a person's idea; the idea then persists as the organization's guiding principle. Throughout its life the organization stimulates people to produce new ideas which, in turn, determine change, all within the bounds of the founding principle. Ideas and organizations thus work together to produce not only change, but orderly change, improvement, correction of flaws, and adjustment to changing environments. A history of the organization reveals ideas that were exemplary and ones that were duds, ideas that met long-term needs and those that met short-term ones, the modest ideas and the ones with wide ramifications, those with glowing potential which ended in disaster and the ones with dubious promise which ended successfully. And finally, every organization has its reserve of ideas that are waiting for their time to come.

The method described in this guidebook stimulates the generation of new ideas and ensures development of ideas to the point where they will be put to work in serving the individuals who produced them and their institutions.

A COOPERATIVE APPROACH TO DEVELOPING IDEAS

Working primarily with large and small liberal arts colleges, we have had many years of experience with the entire process of developing ideas: planning projects, preparing proposals, administering grants, and achieving goals. We have also gained first-hand familiarity with the process as it operates in larger educational institutions and in community service organizations. Along with success, we have known failure.

We have seen a wide range of reference material, conferences with representatives of funding agencies, and workshops, all concerned with just one, or maybe a few, aspects of the process of development of ideas—and this, perhaps, is the clue to the rationale of this publication. The process of developing ideas is all too often separated into segments of the whole instead of being dealt with as an entire process; a great majority of "how to" guides or workshops focus only on one or two of the segments (e.g., preparation of a proposal, sources of funds, or administration of grants), and many institutions parcel out these segments in the same fashion when developing an idea.

The practice of parceling out does permit several functions of the process to go on simultaneously, an attractive method if time is of primary importance. There are, however, serious weaknesses to be weighed against this one advantage. When pieces of work are done independently, most of the benefits resulting from integrated, comprehensive planning are sacrificed, such as the sharing of ideas and experiences. A working partnership among participants is the surest way to avoid pitfalls and to produce a good proposal. If a working partnership is not established, those in charge of the different segments may forget or misinterpret the original idea and are ignorant of changes as the idea develops; they forfeit the opportunity of guiding the growth of the idea during its formative stages, of educating each other in the creative and supportive activities applied during all stages, and of providing their own insights during the constant evaluative process. How often, for instance, have development officers misrepresented an idea when conferring with funding agencies? How often has a faculty member muddled the budget when preparing a proposal? How often has a site visit been snarled up because an administrative officer has been ignorant of the project? The constant evaluative system proposed here will help to avoid those problems.

The idea that develops most successfully is not fragmented but, like a developing organism, retains its integrity throughout an orderly developmental process that has well-marked stages and critical points. Our method reduces or eliminates obstructionist attitudes and procedures and accentuates cooperative ones, secures not only the involvement but the commitment of all participants, and stimulates each participant to contribute at every stage of development; the process is thus educational for all and encourages the articulation and implementation of more ideas.

The most fertile ground for the emergence of ideas is in that segment of the organization most directly concerned with the mission of the organization. The teachers in an educational institution, the nurses in a visiting nurse's association, the artists in a community art center know the problems best and are most likely to find the best solutions. The method described in this guidebook will ensure that the teachers, the nurses, and the artists will not be lost or shunted aside as their ideas develop, and that they will contribute to all stages of development while enjoying an environment that encourages their inventiveness and imagination.

WHO NEEDS THIS GUIDE?

Any individual affiliated with a nonprofit, educational, or service institution who needs assistance in finding additional human, material, and financial resources, whether within or from outside the institution, should benefit from the method described Part I of this guide, and will find varied and useful information in Part II: Basic Resources. Help for the individual will also be of value to the institution. The type of nonprofit institution we refer to is best described by the Internal Revenue Service, and we quote from a digest of the IRS code prepared by the Lutheran Resources Commission, Washington, DC, as follows:

> The Internal Revenue Service requires that an organization seeking to qualify for exemption from Federal income taxes under section 501(c)(3) must file information which will show, among other things, that:
>
> 1. The organization is organized exclusively for, and will be operated exclusively for, one or more of the following purposes: Charitable, Testing for public safety, Religious, Literary, Scientific, Education or Prevention of cruelty to children or animals.
> 2. No part of its net earnings will inure to the benefit of private shareholders or individuals; and
> 3. It will not, as a substantial part of its activities, attempt to influence legislation, or participate to any extent in a

political campaign for or against any candidate for public office.

Because of our experience, we will use the small liberal arts college as our example of an institution, but we could as legitimately use any other nonprofit organization, such as the local historical society or the Visiting Nurse Association. Our natural inclination for this example is reinforced by today's crisis in education, which has had a serious impact on small colleges. These colleges have traditionally proven to be producers of ideas, innovators, and experimenters, particularly in periods of social turbulence. Unlike the large, prestigious institutions, however, they were slow to discover ways of securing the assistance that was made so abundantly available during World War II and later, particularly in the '60s. Now that small colleges, too, have found ways of securing aid the springs are drying up. They must learn to meet stiff competition for assistance, which ranges all the way from advice on better ways to use the already available human, material, and financial resources to the awarding of grants for establishing new programs. This guide, we hope, will bring together institutions needing help and agencies whose function it is to supply help, never forgetting that the essential element in the process is showing the imaginative individual what to do to turn dream into reality.

Origin and Early Development of an Idea

ROLE AND RESPONSIBILITY OF THE INSTITUTION

The institution must recognize that ideas are its life blood, that although there is no way of predicting where ideas will emerge, the most rewarding ones are most likely to arise from that group most closely associated with the mission of the institution. While we can provide no prescription guaranteeing idea production, our general observations suggest that the most favorable milieu is one marked by freedom, lack of barriers between segments of the institution, informality, open doors, and a strong commitment to the institutional goals. Each institution must find its own yeast, but should make it clear that ideas are valued whether or not they are adopted and developed.

HOW TO DEVELOP AN IDEA

The Originator of the idea is the key person in the process discussed in this book. Without an idea nothing will happen. We quote some views on how to develop an idea from a paper by Dr. St. Elmo Naumann, author of several books on philosophy and former professor of Philosophy at Christopher Newport College of the College of William and Mary and most recently serving in the U.S. Navy. The paper was give at a workshop at Lynchburg College in Virginia in 1972 and was presented to the authors for use in this book.

> An idea is an invention. It must be related to a problem which it solves (this may be an intellectual problem). The more important the problem, the more important the idea.

Ways of developing an idea:

1. Read the most authoritative sources until you come to the point where the sources disagree! At that point, you are in a position to make a discovery of your own.
2. Talk with the leading figures in your field. Attend their lectures and ask them careful (and difficult) questions. Ask what their next project is going to be. This may tell you what direction research is going to take.
3. Write the most significant thinkers, if they are too far removed for you to see. If you ask them (courteously) a knowledgeable question, the reply will indicate the direction their thought is taking on the problem at issue.
4. Translate a significant article or book not generally known in this country. The interaction between a new perspective and more familiar ways of thinking may suggest a new path for research. Even administrators can make use of the method of translation.
5. Contemplate your own experience. If there is a frustration blocking your way to fulfillment, you may be able to invent a solution with wider application. "To believe that what is true for you, in your private heart, is true for all mankind: that is the essence of genius." Trust your own instincts.
6. Hurry! If you don't want that new idea, someone else does. The discovery will be made by someone. "Live life as though it were a cavalry charge."

Dr. Naumann's philosophy is simple. No one will force you to have an idea nor to express your idea to others. Read about your subject and talk to others about it. Don't work in secret. Again in his words, "Your aim should be to know more about your subject than anyone else in the world."

ROLE AND RESPONSIBILITIES OF THE ORIGINATOR OF AN IDEA

After coming up with an idea, the Originator will instinctively imagine steps in the idea's development, the extent to which the idea will solve the basic problem, the extent to which it will create new problems, and the way in which those to be affected by the idea will respond to it. If the idea stands up to this period of self-evaluation, it will be described to others. Up to this point, the Originator has sole control of the idea and of how far details should be worked out before the idea is shared. The Originator should recognize however, that the idea, once shared, will affect the thoughts and lives of others. The Originator must anticipate who will be affected if the idea develops, how they will be affected, and what role each person will play in the process. The Originator should compose a list of those most likely to be affected and, at what seems the most propitious moment, share the idea with one of them, probably the department head, and seek advice on the next steps. The people to be affected would probably include those whose roles are described in Exhibit 1 below.

Let's assume the proposal has been submitted and its development approved for funding. The Originator then notifies all concerned in the project, making sure that all the participants understand their roles; the goals, freedoms, and limitations in each role; and the manner in which separate goals will ultimately fit to make an integrated whole.

The Originator must then supervise all portions of the project while keeping the overall goal in clear focus. He or she must also see that all records are kept, particularly that meticulous, day-by-day financial records are available at all times and that expenditures are consistent with line items in the proposal.

As the project develops, changes in the original plans are almost inevitable, for an idea doesn't stop growing or changing just because it has been described and its implementation has been funded. Participants discover new possibilities or find unexpected pitfalls; personnel changes and the resulting changes in areas of expertise call for adjustments; inflated costs of equipment prohibit some procedures. It is the Originator's responsibility to weigh alternatives and, if necessary, request that certain changes be permitted.

The Originator will be responsible for the momentum of the project, for setting and meeting deadlines, and for maintaining morale among the group. In other words, the Originator becomes the Project Director.

SPECIFIC PEOPLE AND THEIR TASKS

Who are the people the Orginator needs to notify? They probably would be those listed in Exhibit 1, depending upon which of the three types of organization applies. As we proceed, you can adjust this chart to fit the titles in your organization. It should be recognized at the outset that institutional projects mean change, and change inevitably entails major and minor adjustments, compromises, and realignments of priorities. Though one person articulates the idea that grows into a project, full development of the project requires aid from those who will be affected by it, those trained to deal with special facets of its development, and those responsible for making change an orderly and constructive process.

Ideally, the various people assisting in a project provide support and enthusiasm, and understand each other's roles and views so well that success is assured. This group is the single most potent factor serving the harmony, effectiveness, and ultimate success of the developing project. The most severe threat to a project's success is failure to communicate within the group.

To avoid failure, therefore, all affected people should meet regularly throughout the life of the project, not only during the preliminary stages.

Originator of the Idea/Project Director

The Originator must share the idea, probably, first with the Department Chair, then with that individual responsible for guiding and coordinating plans. The Grants/Sponsored Programs Officer is the person we will describe in this role of "coordinator." The Chair and Grants Officer, assuming they express approval and willingness to cooperate, will advise the Originator on procedures. Some of the procedures will undoubtedly relate to the academic or professional aspects of the project, others to the logistical or managerial aspects. Procedural failure in either category, resulting in poor communication, delays, and irritations, can often kill a plan almost before it has seen the light of day.

The next duty of the Originator will be to describe the idea to appropriate colleagues and administrative officers. Together, all of these people will become the group that will aid the Originator in guiding the plan throughout its life. Originators may have many unexpected tasks to

Exhibit 1. Titles of People Involved in the Development of Ideas.

Higher Education Agency	Community Agency	Health Care
Department Chair	Supervisor	Division Director
Department Members	Staff Members	Nurses/Doctors
Academic Dean	Organization Director	Executive Director/Administrator
Chief Fiscal Officer	Chief Fiscal Officer	Chief Fiscal Officer
Chancellor/President	Board Chair	Board Chair
Grants/Sponsored Programs Officer	Fund Raiser/Development Officer	Fund Raiser/Development Officer

perform, but one thing is certain—they will have to stay with their projects from start to finish and be responsible for making or approving all substantive changes as the plans evolve.

Department Chair

The Department Chair is in the best position to judge the merits of a plan in terms of feasibility, desirability, and possible ramifications within the department. In weighing the plan, the Chair must also assess the kinds of encouragement and constructive contributions to be counted on from the department. It goes without saying that a department head wishes to encourage the professional development of all department members and thus, when a plan proposed by one of these members is approved, will take whatever steps are necessary to see the project through to completion. The steps would include planning time and resources if the project calls for changes in schedules and staffing, and balancing the new plan with other ongoing departmental projects. The Department Chair, whether a member of the group guiding the new project or not, must be familiar with the details in order to help solve problems of time and personnel, to converse effectively with representatives of funding agencies on site visits, and to interpret the significance of the new project to those outside the department. Once the proposed idea is approved, the Chair will combine whatever talents of diplomacy, persuasion, and understanding she or he may have in securing positive responses from those who will be directly or indirectly related to the success of the project.

Department Members

Depending on areas of specialization, talents, general interests, and available time in their schedules, Members may be called on to fill major or minor roles in a developing project as one of their departmental tasks; they should accept such responsibilities as a normal part of life within a department and expect the Chair to plan suitable adjustments if the new duties jeopardize their other responsibilities.

Academic Dean

The Academic Dean, or the person responsible for leadership in planning the academic program, being the officer with the most comprehensive understanding of the entire instructional program, will inevitably be intimately involved with any new idea affecting the curriculum and teaching staff. Insights gained in the office enable the Dean to judge not only the feasibility and desirability of a new academic venture in the context of institutional goals, but also to provide expert advice on procedure, timing, human resources, and economy of effort during the entire period of development. The Dean will also help describe the plan to the representatives of funding agencies when they make site visits and to interested faculty, students, and visiting graduates and parents.

Chief Fiscal Officer

The Chief Fiscal Officer is one person completely familiar with all details of the institution's finances. A new project requires resources, including financial resources. The money, whether found within the institution or sought from outside, must be considered in reference to the institutional budget. The Fiscal Officer is responsible for considering all financial facets of the new program, including matching money, cost-sharing, indirect costs, Social Security payments, and record keeping for audit. Schedules for outlay of funds and requests for payment must also be made by the finance office.

President/Chancellor

The President reinforces some of the contributions of the Fiscal Officer and Dean, and is the person who speaks officially for the institution, bearing the overall responsibility for its vigor and the success of new developments. If funds are sought from an outside source, it is the President, or in some cases a Vice President or Provost, who signs the proposal and, if the proposal is accepted, the final contract. The President may deputize a representative to the group guiding the idea's growth but ultimately should be familiar with the final proposal.

Grants/Sponsored Programs Officer

If financial assistance is sought from outside the institution, it will be the Grants Officer who decides which agencies would be appropriate sources. This officer will undoubtedly assist in preparing a proposal and often, before submitting a proposal, will visit or make contact with selected agencies to discover whether or not they would be interested in the project. It is important, therefore, that this officer should understand not only the nature of the project but also the ways in which a realization of the project's goals would benefit the institution. The Grants Officer can prepare for the tasks of composing and presenting a proposal only by participating in the whole process of planning.

If the institution has no grants officer on its staff to coordinate the kind of planning being described, it should designate such a person. In most of the institutions with which we are familiar, it is the person responsible for sponsored programs who is the logical coordinator, because this person's work with sponsored programs and research requires coordination of academic, development, and administrative spheres. The Grants Officer, a catalyst, should have a talent for making things happen, convening an appropriate mix of participants, timing, establishing momentum and maintaining pace, setting deadlines, facilitating mechanics of the planning procedure, taking initiative, ensuring communication among participants, and avoiding pitfalls. In short, the Grants Officer should be gear greaser, diplomat, politician, source of information, and gadfly all in one. Without someone to coordinate the effort, the plans will limp or bog down, deadlines will be missed, serendipitous opportunities will pass unnoticed, frictions will develop, and participants will fail to appreciate their own and other's roles.

The Grants Officer will probably be the first person after the Department Chair to discuss the plan with the Originator and to assess its feasibility. From the moment of approval, the Grants Officer will be the chief agent in guiding development of the idea and guarding its integrity, in assisting the Originator in every way, and in helping to prepare a proposal. If a grant is received, the Grants Officer will guide the project director and all the participants in administering the grant and proceeding to the desired goals.

The most pressing responsibilities of the Grants Officer are in the process of proposal development—planning and scheduling work so that the proposal will be ready for internal approval in time to meet the deadline for submitting it to the selected funding agency. Early in the process the Grants Officer should prepare a timetable to cover the entire period.

THE SYSTEM OF DEVELOPMENT BEGINS TO OPERATE

The Originator, having been encouraged by the Chair and the Grants Officer, puts the idea on paper together with a brief abstract of the plan, its cost, the resources required, and a list of those whose help will be needed. The Grants Officer convenes those identified by the Originator (the same people whose anticipated roles were described earlier). It is important that there be an actual meeting rather than circulation of a paper because, for the good of the project, those concerned need to interact, to hear the comments and criticisms of others. This meeting becomes the first general exercise in evaluation and determines whether or not plans should proceed. Assuming the idea is judged worth pursuing, the group considers details of the plan, what further information is needed, what steps should be taken and when, and other important questions: Does the idea so affect the academic program that the academic policy committee should be notified? Does the plan require approval from some committee or office? Does it commit the institution to such a fundamental change in concept of the institution's mission that the President should notify the Board? Does it infer a financial commitment or obligation, either additional funds or ongoing costs? Does it require matching funds or cost-sharing? "Matching funds" means finding a dollar-for-dollar match in hard cash. "Cost-sharing" may mean contributions in kind, in time, space, materials, or the contribution of indirect costs. Both are financial commitments. Are there others outside the group whose help will be needed? If so, their willingness to assist must be determined, and permission to use their names must be secured.

The first business of the meeting will be to block out a realistic schedule to serve as a basis for the Grants Officer's timetable, which will detail all deadlines up to and including the date of submission of the proposal. The first item on the timetable will be the securing of approvals and willingness to help from all parties. The timetable will include allowance for delays, and ideally will provide a comfortable interval between the date set for completion of the proposal and the deadline date for its submission. Even though the Grants officer has checked the travel schedule of those whose signatures are required on the completed document (the Fiscal Officer and the President), accumulated delays and unforeseen exigencies can turn this interval into a critical or even hectic period. Never expect the funding agency to extend its deadline.

At the close of the first meeting immediate tasks will have been assigned to members of the group, roles of members will have begun to take shape, and chief target dates will be clear. The Grants Officer should prepare timetables starting with a six-month timetable for the distribution of drafts to meet the submission deadline and follow up with a more detailed timetable for each month prior to the submission deadline. (See Exhibits 2 and 3.) These serve as planning and reminding documents.

Exhibit 2. Six-Month Timetable.

JUNE	JULY	AUGUST	SEPTEMBER	OCTOBER	NOVEMBER	DECEMBER
15th Meeting to discuss idea with those affected						
	15th Develop details of plan for internal comment Draft 1					
		15th Revise to reflect comments received Draft 2				
			Circulate Draft 2			
				15th Revise to reflect comments Final Draft 3		
					Circulate Final Draft 3 for approval	
						Dec. 1 Submit Proposal Prior to deadline

Exhibit 3. Activity Schedule/Status Report.

Date	Activity	Status
June 1	meet with Department Head to discuss idea	
June 6	meet with Coordinator to get logistical help and get idea on paper	Abstract on paper
June 15	meet with all those affected by idea to discuss idea and seek encouragement	
June 15-July 15	develop detailed plan for circulation to those who met June 15	Draft #1
July 15	circulate draft for committee by August 1, enlist campus participants	
Aug. 1-Sept. 1	respond to comments and prepare Draft #2 for comments--those who will participate will revise draft	Draft #2
Sept. 1-15	circulate Draft #2 to those affected and those enlisted; comment by October 1	
Oct. 2-15	revise and work out changes with those affected	Revision Draft #2
Oct. 15-Nov. 1	prepare final draft for approval, in form for duplicating	Final Draft
Nov. 1-15	circulate final revisions	Circulate Final Draft
Nov. 15-20	final approvals, assurances; submission papers collected and required number of copies duplicated and assembled	
Nov. 20	signature of Chief Fiscal Officer	
Nov. 21	signature of President	
Nov. 22	finished proposal packaged and mailed or delivered to meet deadline	Submission

The Proposal : A Design for Putting an Idea to Work

WHAT IS IN A SOUND PROPOSAL?

General Considerations

Plans for implementing the initial idea inevitably lead to an outline, then to a rough draft of a proposal. The individual or individuals composing successive drafts should constantly strive for a thoroughly detailed and clearly articulated description of the needs that must be satisfied for fulfillment of the initial idea. The needs must be clearly consistent with institutional and departmental goals, not contrived to match uses specified by a potential funding source. Remember that the role of the Grants Officer is to discover a funding source whose interests include those described in the proposal. (This is not to say that a brochure from a funding source might not trigger a good idea, which, of course, would then be described with that particular source in mind.)

The next step is to turn the rough draft into a sound proposal, realizing that before submission a proposal will gradually undergo major and minor changes as the idea grows and as the participating group examines it critically. Preparation of a formal proposal is a valuable exercise whether or not the proposal is to be submitted to a funding agency, because the process helps to clarify ideas, to point up weaknesses, and to help nonparticipating colleagues understand the idea and the contemplated project. Furthermore, those who authorize internal support and make official commitments to support the project should be as demanding as an outside funding agency in requiring detailed plans. A proposal should, therefore, be prepared whether or not it is to be sent outside the institution.

Assuming that outside support is to be sought and an appropriate agency has been selected, the proposal must be adjusted to conform to the agency's guidelines. All sources ask for basically the same information, and it is exactly the kind of information already gathered if preliminary planning has been properly carried out. We mention this because one block or misunderstanding that turns people away from proposal writing is the notion that no two sources of funding ask for the same information. Though the general format of a proposal varies little among agencies, descriptive terms referring to sections of the proposal may vary. We reviewed guidelines from a wide variety of agencies and foundations and collected terms used for the various components of a proposal. The order in which information was requested varied. Topics were the same, regardless of terminology. Exhibit 4 lists various parallel terms used for the contents of a proposal.

Exhibit 4. Components of a Typical Proposal with Variations in Terminology.

MOST COMMON HEADING	VARIATIONS
Cover Sheet	Application Form, Title Page
Table of Contents	
Abstract	Summary, Executive Summary
Problem Statement	Statement of Need, Questions to be Addressed
Goals	General Objectives, Solutions
Measurable Objectives	Specific Objectives, Expected Outcomes
Procedures	Activities, Narrative, Operating Plans, Action Plan, Research Design, Strategies
Evaluation	Formative and Summative Evaluation, Instrumentation for Assessment, Assessment of Outcomes
Dissemination	Transferability, Distribution of Results, Utilization Plan, Replicability
Facilities	Space and Equipment Requirements
Personnel	Capability of Staff, Special Competencies
Budget	Fiscal Requirements, Project Costs, Financial Resources
Appendices	Background Material, Supporting Documents

Keep in mind that preparation of a formal and final proposal is one part of a process; it must follow the initial identification of need and description of an idea, and the subsequent development of the idea, formulation of plans to implement it, and establishment of priorities. A successful proposal is the culminating event of an orderly, thorough, and thoughtful developmental process. In fact, the principal fault we find with most of the literature and seminars on proposal writing is that the task is not considered within the total context of the developing idea.

Much has been written on proposal writing from a management standpoint. People tend not to think of the process of developing an idea as a "management system," but the process—including motivation, design, implementation, assessment, administration, reporting, and final audit—is, in fact, a management system. We found much helpful information in the National Science Foundation's Research Management Improvement Program and in the internal policy manuals shared by administrators in other institutions. Methods of motivating those with ideas and systems for matching faculty capability with sources of support for their research have been developed by these groups in ways we found particularly useful and applicable to small institutions.

Developing the final proposal should still be preceded by outlines and a series of drafts that have been gradually improved and refined, satisfying the critical judgment of all participants. The drafts may also serve as the clearest exposition of the developing plan for those directly or indirectly affected by the plan at various times during the process of development. Greater coherence and orderliness in the proposal may be achieved if you think of it as a set of instructions for someone to carry out; you must realize that a final, polished version may be many drafts away. Never underestimate the value of the drafts, for they will be the means of securing internal support which, of course, must precede the seeking of external support.

An abstract or summary of the proposal should also be prepared, whether or not it is specified in guidelines; it is a useful document, particularly for the Grants Officers as they seek suitable funding agencies. The abstract, a distillation of the entire proposal, should occupy no more than two pages; it must be carefully and concisely constructed, and must include all of the major features of the project, especially how it will satisfy needs and the anticipated cost. A "preliminary proposal," sometimes requested by a funding agency, should provide the same kind of information as an abstract but can include more details and descriptive material. We emphasize again that however brief the abstract or preliminary proposal, all major elements must be included.

The Specific Parts of a Proposal

The headings appearing below, and the appropriate information that goes with them, should be used even during your earliest preparation, because they will correspond in major respects to most guideline instructions. This procedure will spare you from making extensive revisions when you write the proposal in its final form.

Cover Sheet

Title: The title should be brief but should include the most important words describing the project, preferably the words likely to be picked up by a computer preparing bibliographies, e.g., *Improving Competency of Women in Securing Support for Research*. Then, on the same page, give the following information:

Submitted by: Name and Degree

Address

Rank

Institution

Address

Date: (Date of submission)

N. B. (1) If an agency provides a cover sheet form, use it. This will then serve as your title page and must therefore be the first item in the proposal.

(2) We assume a proposal will have a letter of transmittal and endorsement. This is discussed in the section on submission.

Table of Contents

This should follow the Cover Sheet and should include section headings and subheadings with the page where each one starts. Be sure that the headings in contents match those in the body of your proposal.

Abstract

Write the Abstract last. This may be your most important and most difficult effort, as its quality will determine whether or not the reader examines the rest of the proposal. Write a simple summary of what is to be accomplished, how it will be accomplished, how the project will be evaluated, who will benefit from it and how, and what it will cost. This should fill no more than two pages. We repeat: Tell all, but be concise. An abstract for a hypothetical proposal to the National Endowment for the Humanities follows below.

Problem Statement

The idea worth developing is the one answering a recognized need. State the need or problem clearly. Don't exaggerate it or give it dimensions beyond the scope of the proposal or the competence of those involved. Take to heart a warning that appeared in an article published by the American Association of State Colleges and Universities (AASCU), "Don't take on the problems of the universe." Focus sharply on the problem in such a way that the limits of the problem and its solution become clear. Following the example used earlier under Cover Sheet, the need could be stated as follows: *Women have not had equal opportunity and assistance necessary to secure grant support.*

Exhibit 5. Abstract.

Institution: Northwest State University, Taxville, WA
Type of institution: State University
No. of students: 15,000
Type of grant: Planning
Inclusive dates of grant: 1/1/76-3/31/77
Project Title: Northwest Coast Studies Program
Project Director: Arthur Foresight
Amt. requested: $27,532

OBJECTIVES: Through NEH funds the departments of Anthropology, Art, History, and English, in cooperation with the staff of the Fells Museum, will develop an undergraduate concentration in Northwest Coast Studies. This program will offer an intellectual focus to departments that presently offer a large but fragmented set of courses and suffer declining enrollments. We propose, therefore, to offer one new course in each department, an interdisciplinary junior-senior seminar on culture change in the Northwest, an undergraduate internship at the Fells Museum, and a research colloquium for students and staff concerned with Northwest Coast Studies. This program will build on the research interests of 5 of 14 members of these combined departments, expand the use of the Fells collection and summer archaeology program, and promote a more meaningful interaction between the departments cited. Our goals are to strengthen the quality of instruction, increase student sensitivity to the interrelationship of disciplines, and to increase enrollment in upper-level history and anthropology courses.

TIMETABLE: Anthropology will offer a sophomore level course "Indians of the Northwest" in the fall of 1976; in the spring of 1977, History will offer "Northwest from 1750" and English will offer "Literature of the Northwest." A select group of 6 sophomores will begin 10 hr/wk museum internships in this semester. The summer program will be a continuation of the museum archaeological program. We will continue the sophomore sequence in the fall. In addition, Art will offer "Art and Architecture of the Northwest." Four teachers will offer a junior-senior interdisciplinary seminar on "Culture Change in the Northwest" and the Humanities Program will sponsor the research symposium "Recent Scholarship on the Northwest." In 1977 two courses will be dropped from the curriculum: "History of Latin America" and "Ethnography of Appalachia."

TEACHING STRATEGIES: Departmental offerings will be taught as lectures. The seminar will be taught by two members each of History and Anthropology with occasional assistance from Music, English, and Art. Interns at the museum will be assigned to the curator or the assistant curator who will supervise their project in cooperation with a faculty advisor. The seminar, symposium, and museum programs will draw on faculty and students from the departments of Linguistics, Religion, Botany, and Geology.

FACULTY: Dean Foresight, Project Director; H. Herodotus, Ch., Dept. of Hist., & B. Boas, Ch., Dept. of Anthro.; Project Co-chair, Prf. Fulcrum, Dept. of Hist. & Anthro; S. Potter, Curator; P. Wissler, Ass't Curator; Prof. Baal, Hist.; A. Jenson, Art; W. Shakespeare, Engl.

EVALUATION: Four kinds of evaluation will be used: enrollment data, use of interdisciplinary facilities and number of interdisciplinary projects undertaken by faculty and students, faculty evaluation by a committee not involved in the program, and outside evaluation by Franz Salmon and J. Totem, leading Northwest Coast scholars.

Goals and Objectives

An examination of various guidelines indicates that two kinds of objectives usually need to be stated; the first, often called "goal," being more general, inclusive, and describable in qualitative terms; the second, a series of specific expectations describable in quantitative terms and serving the first general objective or goal.

The title suggested above would then be followed by:

Goal: to improve the competency of women in securing financial support for research projects in their particular fields

Objectives: to enroll 25 women Ph. D.'s with no experience in applying for grants in a workshop and train them to the point where each can plan and design a project and describe it in the form of a proposal that would be judged competitive in terms of Office of Education review criteria, and to accomplish the objective in a three-week summer training program.

The greatest weakness in proposals probably appears in the statement of objectives. Grandiose ideas whose expected outcomes are not measurable in quantitative or qualitative terms are too often the rule. When you set forth your objectives, list them, and consider carefully how you would measure or judge the success of each.

Procedures

Strictures on this section are less severe than on others, though our general advice is to write simply and clearly and according to a logical outline. Strive for a maximum of "protein" in your writing, a minimum of "carbohydrate" and "fat." Avoid esoteric and technical terms unless you are assured that readers and reviewers will be familiar with them. Avoid "buzz" or "in" words—by the time your proposal is read, they will probably be "out." Avoid flowery prose.

The following excerpts and comments date back almost two decades and are still valid today. The kind of writing that is offensive in a proposal is apparently the same kind deplored by *Newsweek*:

> Nowhere has the art of obfuscation been more refined than in the drawing up of administrative proposals. Lloyd Kaplan, information officer of the New York City Planning Commission, has made a hobby of analyzing the technique. "Proposals," he reports, "are habitually placed in *frameworks* so that they can be viewed from the proper *perspective*. Looking through the framework, it is easy to chart appropriate *guidelines*. Such guidelines are *flexible* and handy for making *bold thrusts, dramatic approaches* and *pioneering breakthroughs*." "Money," continues Kaplan is never mentioned. "*Resources* is the prime substitute, although *expenditures, allocations, appropriations* and *funds* are also popular. *Resources* is also esthetically pleasing because it brings to mind the act of digging up and forms a truly Miltonic phrase when preceded by 'over-burdened municipal.' "

John Hightower, at the New York State Council on the Arts in the 1970s, is another perceptive student of proposal making. In requisitioning money, says Hightower, "the cardinal rule is never to employ the word 'subsidy,' since it implies one is asking for complete funding. In place of subsidy, inventive politicians . . . have taken to using 'subvention.'" These comments were made 20 years ago. The writing they describe has gone from bad to worse. Heed their advice and avoid these types of words.

A second rule is to fluff up a proposal with the sort of euphemisms that bestow an aura of importance without revealing anything specific. An application for a federal grant from a small southern California college illustrates the technique. Describing a proposed project, the applicant states: "It is not simply a cross-disciplinary venture or an inter-disciplinary venture; it is a pan-disciplinary venture and this, of course, is in the nature of all real experience."

The ultimate in sure-fire-how-to-write-a-loser is set forth in the following game. This game has been copied and passed around agencies and foundations for over 15 years and continues to cause snickers and elicit stories about bad proposal writing.

How to Win at Wordsmanship

After hacking for years through etymological thickets at the U.S. Public Health Service, a 63-year-old official named Philip Broughton hit upon a sure-fire method for converting frustration into fulfillment (jargon-wise). Euphemistically called the Systematic Buzz Phrase Projector, Broughton's system employs a lexicon of 30 carefully chosen "buzzwords":

Column 1	Column 2	Column 3
0. integrated	0. management	0. options
1. total	1. organizational	1. flexibility
2. systematized	2. monitored	2. capability
3. parallel	3. reciprocal	3. mobility
4. functional	4. digital	4. programming
5. responsive	5. logistical	5. concept
6. optional	6. transitional	6. time-phase
7. synchronized	7. incremental	7. projection
8. compatible	8. third-generation	8. hardware
9. balanced	9. policy	9. contingency

The procedure is simple. Think of any three-digit number, then select the corresponding buzzword from each column. For instance, number 257 produced "systematized logistical projection," a phrase that can be dropped into virtually any report with that ring of decisive, knowledgeable authority. "No one will have the remotest idea of what you're talking about," says Broughton, "but the important thing is that they're not about to admit it."

Clear writing is important because the procedures section is where you explain how you plan to do the things set forth in your objectives, when you plan to do the work, how long it will take, who else will be working on the project, exactly what they will be doing and where they will be doing it, and what will be needed in facilities, equipment, supplies, time, and personnel. Be specific.

Describe your institution and the competence of both the institution and the people to complete the objectives. Explain what will happen to the project when the funds are spent, and the extent to which this project may dovetail with other ongoing projects, or pave the way for future plans.

Continuing with the example suggested in the Cover Sheet and Objectives sections, we illustrate the kind of detailed plan that should appear in your Procedures.

The first thing to do is list the steps you will take, when you will start each activity, who will do the work, where it will be done, when it will be completed, and what it will cost in time and materials. (See Exhibit 6.)

Continue this procedure to include the entire project. Once you have completed such a schedule of activities, describe each activity in detail with appropriate charts and references. For example, if we turn to the June 15th activity we should find:

> The initial activity in the training program will be a one-day workshop designed to illustrate the roles and relationships of the various persons affected by an idea. A Dean, Business Officer, Development Officer, Grant Manager, and Faculty Member with experience as a department head and success in securing grants will be teamed with representatives of government, private, and corporate funding sources to address the topics outlined for the workshop. These persons will be recruited from outside the faculty of the training program.

The method prescribed in this book for the development of the idea is the basis for the workshop and the training program detailed in this sample proposal. An outline for the first session of the workshop is shown in Exhibit 7.

The design for this workshop on proposal development is such that it can be readily adapted to different settings and interest groups. It is important that at least two of the instructors have a thorough understanding of the process we are describing. Each new combination of persons recruited to represent the roles of the Originator, Department Head, Administrator, and Grants Officer can interpolate the views represented in the group into the roles mentioned earlier.

We suggest that this workshop serve as a training session for the representatives of the colleges, universities, and community agencies in attendance and as an example of an exercise that can be performed at their home institutions when projects are being developed.

Evaluation

An essential inclusion in any proposal is a statement on evaluation: how the developing idea and proposal and, finally, the completed project will be assessed. Funding agencies often ask how the evaluative process will be conducted and require reports on the process itself and on the conclusions drawn by those administering the project. Even if an agency doesn't ask for an evaluation, you should have an evaluation system for your own and your institution's benefit.

Exhibit 6. Detailed List of Activities.

Jan. 5	Develop an application form for the training program
Feb. 1	Distribute application to 200 institutions; set Feb. 20 as deadline for receiving applications
Mar. 1-Mar. 15	Screen applications and select 30 who will provide range in type of institution, interests, and geographic location
Mar. 20	Notify applicants
April-May	Produce in final form the list of materials to be used in the program (outlines, topical papers, bibliographies, etc.), and the budget; [this will help you in drafting a final budget.]
	4 working-weeks $1,500
	Secretarial help 100
	Postage 50
	Publications 100
June 15	Opening of workshop
	Directors 200
	Consultants, 5 @ $100/day
	& travel @ $100 1,000
	Materials 300

Exhibit 7. Workshop Outline.

The purpose of this workshop is to expose the audience and the participants to the interrelatedness of the roles of the many persons affected by an idea and will demonstrate how effective use of the process will lead to a sound proposal.

Workshop on Proposal Development and Grant Opportunities for Individuals, Departmental and Institutional Projects

8: 30	REGISTRATION, COFFEE AND DANISH	
9: 15	WELCOME & INTRODUCTION OF PARTICIPANTS	
9: 30	OUTLINE OF DAY'S ACTIVITIES	Workshop Director

Presentation on Process of the Development of an Idea

9: 45	PANEL: FROM IDEA TO THE WRITTEN PROPOSAL	
	The Idea Originator	Professor Green
	The Head of the Department	Professor Smith
	The Administration	Dean Jones
	The Grants Officer	Ms. Reed
	The Funding Organization	Dr. Black

Five-minute presentation by each participant to describe his or her role in developing an idea with the remaining thirty-five minutes for questions.

10: 45	COFFEE BREAK	
11: 00	FUNDING ORGANIZATIONS	
Private Foundations		Dr. Black
Corporation Foundations		Mr. Davis
Government Agencies		Dr. Bird

Three 15-minute presentations covering:

a) what each foundation, corporation, or agency funds

b) what each expects in a proposal

c) how each judges a proposal

An open discussion will follow on the similarities and differences among the 3 groups.

12: 15	BREAK FOR LUNCH	
1: 15	THE INGREDIENTS OF A PROPOSAL	Workshop Director

The Director will address the	Dr. Black
subject in outline form. A	Dr. Bird
panel is made up of one grants	Ms. Reed
officer, one funding agency representative,	
and a third person from among the outside participants.	

3: 00	PEER PANEL REVIEW	

A submitted proposal will be	Dr. Black
reviewed by a panel convened	Dr. Bird
for this purpose. Copies of this	Professor Smith
proposal will now be distributed	Professor Green
to all participants. One funding source	3 trainees
representative will serve as convenor.	
Panel will include 3 outside participants	
and 3 trainees.	

3: 45	CONCLUSIONS OF THE PANEL WILL BE DISCUSSED	Dr. Black
4: 00	ACTUAL REVIEW OF THE PROPOSAL	Workshop Director
4: 30	ADJOURN	

We deal with evaluation more fully in "Tests for Soundness of a Proposal" rather than here because the topic includes more than just the description of the evaluation process needed for developing the proposal. Evaluation of a project is increasingly important to the grantor. It is so important that we have included a separate section with an example evaluation following the grant administration section.

Dissemination

Proposals often state that the project is a "pilot study," or that the results would be useful to other institutions. If the latter is the case, how will the results, materials, and projects or plans be made available to others, and how will the transfer be implemented? These questions should be carefully considered before answers are given. Be realistic and practical in anticipating what can and will be done. Funding sources may press for answers to the transferability question in such a way that the proposer is tempted to contrive an answer. Don't be tempted. If a dissemination plan is required by a funding source and such a plan is not appropriate for your proposal, it is wiser not to apply to this source.

Your project, on the other hand, may have some very clear implications in terms of its applicability elsewhere, or it may already be adapted to dissemination with no difficulty. If you consider a project plan adaptable to another setting, state this in your proposal, explain the means of dissemination and make any necessary provisions in your budget.

Dissemination can be taken care of through a series of workshops or through a publication. The workshop on proposal development, which was described earlier, illustrates a replicable device because the role-playing approach is open to a new set of characters as long as the principle is understood and applied. Publications and materials produced by many good projects, however, fill shelves and gather dust because there was no plan to advertise and make these materials available. For example, it is reasonable to argue that a new method involving computerized instruction could be transferred by making the programs available or by devising a system permitting access to your computer. Nevertheless, it is still necessary to explain in your proposal how you will make this known and how you will handle production and distribution, or accessibility of material requested. We have often written to project directors whose proposals claimed that reports would be made readily available to other institutions only to discover that dissemination ended with 10 to 25 copies because no

provision for distribution had been made in the grant budget or through internal resources.

Facilities

The proposal should include a statement indicating the availability of needed facilities. If, for instance, large audiences are expected for a lecture series or continuing education activities, give information on the space available for the group you expect. Be certain classrooms are free for use and that those who are responsible for assigning space and seeing that the buildings are open know and agree to your requirements. If technical facilities such as audiovisual equipment are not available, be sure to make allowances for these needs in your budget. A proposal describing plans for large community audiences of 500 or more stands no chance of support when the description of facilities indicates that the largest available auditorium holds only 250 people. Be meticulous and thorough in anticipating your needs. The prospective funding source appreciates and respects thorough planning.

Personnel

Give an honest assessment of the extent to which the capabilities of personnel to be involved satisfy requirements of the project. Does the project demand competency in a subject not taught at your institution? If so, explain how you will fill the gap and make any budget allowances necessary. Explain special areas of expertise represented among involved personnel. We are reminded of a proposal submitted by a young instructor in a small institution, requesting a rather sophisticated and complex configuration of apparatus. His proposal would have been turned down because a reviewer questioned whether anyone in such an institution would have enough experience to use such equipment. It was discovered by pure chance that the proposer had been responsible for setting up and maintaining similar equipment as a graduate student. This should have been made clear in the proposal as granting agencies are naturally unwilling to approve investments in equipment that no one knows how to use. When listing the competencies required in the project, do not overlook those needed for some special task. If outsiders must be brought in, explain where you will find the people you want. We suggest that you list by name several such specialists, even though you have no commitment from them. If certain distinguished experts are sought, explain what makes you think you can secure them. Have similar institutions had their services? Are they personal friends, related to a trustee, or known to be willing to come for a particular fee?

The qualifications of your personnel are best supported by the *curriculum vitae* of each, particularly those with key roles in the project. The list would include, of course, the Project Director (P. D.), or the Principal Investigator (P. I.), in a research project, and those with some important specialization spelled out in the proposal. We suggest using a uniform, standard format for the *curriculum vitae,* and we have provided a sample form with instructions in the Basic Resources. If some agency asks for specific information not included in the suggested form, simply add the required information.

Budget

Every item in the budget should be described in the narrative part of the procedures. It is helpful to the reader if the section of the narrative devoted to these brief descriptions lists them in the same sequence in which they appear in the budget. One can also add very brief descriptions to the individual budget items. Every anticipated cost should be listed, adjusted to projected price increases. Do not inflate the budget—too often proposal writers equate an inflated budget with a complete and adequate budget; this is a false assumption. Prepare a reasonable back-up budget for a less costly approach to the project, but do not agree to changes that would jeopardize the success and quality of the project.

The business officer of any organization must approve the budget and sign financial reports. It is this individual who will be most helpful in preparing the budget, particularly in including such items as Social Security withholding figures, which are often overlooked by writers of proposals. The business officer will also know the institution's current indirect cost rate, or, if one has not been recently negotiated with the appropriate federal agency, will develop this figure. Current instructions spelled out in the *National Science Foundation's Grant Administration Manual* or in the *Department of Health and Human Services Indirect Cost Proposals* will provide a basis for calculating indirect costs and institutional contributions until a final rate is negotiated. The rate is usually based on salaries and wages (S+W) but some situations demand a rate based on total direct cost, or separate rates for off-campus or overseas activities. Few private foundations recognize indirect costs or overhead figures. Ask the sponsor, if it is not a government agency, what direct and indirect costs will be allowed before finalizing your budget. For those unfamiliar with the term "indirect cost" or "indirect expenses," we quote from Combined Glossary, Terms and Definitions from the *Handbooks of the State Educational Records and Reports Series, U.S. Department of Health Education and Welfare, Education Division,* 1974. Variations of this statment show up in current publications. This particular wording seemed to be most helpful to the neophyte.

> Those elements of cost necessary in the provision of a service which are of such nature that they cannot be readily or accurately identified with the specific service. For example, the custodial staff may clean corridors in a school building, which is used jointly by administrative, instructional, maintenance and attendance personnel. In this case, a part of the custodial salaries is an indirect expense of each service using the corridors. However, it is impossible to determine readily or accurately the amount of salary to charge each of these services.

The indirect cost figure is important because the claimed indirect costs on a grant may provide your most important, if not the only, means of sharing costs with a funding source. Demonstration of the institution's support of a project is often sought through a requirement to "cost-share." You can share the cost of a project by using indirect cost money for project expenses and by making contributions "in kind," such as support devices, facilities, and supplies. The terms "cost-sharing" and "matching" are not to be confused. "Matching" money is a cash outlay made by the institution according to whatever ratio the funding source sets. Many federal agencies suggest formats and items to be included in the budget. Examining a sample budget used for a funding agency requiring cost sharing is perhaps the best way for a beginner to learn how to develop a budget. The following exhibit is a sample budget that provides a thumbnail sketch of the times and activities which would be described in the narration.

Exhibit 8. Sample Grant Budget.

	SPONSOR	APPLICANT	TOTAL
A. Personnel			
1. Professor Jones, Proj. Dir. 1/2 released time for acad. yr. salary $40,000	$10,000	$10,000	$20,000
2. Professor Smith 1/2 released time Fall semester; salary $36,000	9,000		9,000
3. Professor Brown 1/2 released time Fall semester; salary $30,000		7,500	7,500
4. Professor Green 1/2 released time Spring semester; salary $30,000	7,500		7,500
5. Secretary 1/2 time; salary $14,000	3,500	3,500	7,000
SUBTOTAL - Salaries & Wages	$30,000	$21,000	$51,000
B. Fringe Benefits (22% of S&W)	$6,600	$4,620	$11,220
C. Consultants			
1. Consultants (2 @ $250/day for two days)	1,000		1,000
2. Consultant Travel (2 @ $350 + 2 days x $75 per diem)	1,000		1,000
SUBTOTAL - C	$2,000		$2,000
D. Staff Travel			
1. Professor Jones: 1 trip to U. S. College to observe similar program. 500 mi. x $. 21 per mile = $105. per diem $75 for 3 days = $225.	330		330
2. Professors Smith & Green: 1 trip to National University for (purpose). Plane fare est. $340 for each = $680. $75 per diem for two days each = $300.	980		980
SUBTOTAL - D	$1,310		$1,310
E. Supplies			
1. Institutional materials (slides, tapes)	600	200	800
2. Office supplies (paper, ribbon, etc.)	500	100	600
SUBTOTAL - E	$1,100	$300	$1,400
F. Other			
1. Communications, (telephone, mail, etc.) @ $200/month for 12 months	1,468	932	2,400
2. Equipment rental: 2 tape recorders @ $200 = $400; 1 mm projector @ $150	550		550
3. Library acquistions (attach breakdown)	1,200	800	2,000
SUBTOTAL - F	$3,218	$1,732	$4,950
G. Total Direct Costs	$44,428	$27,652	$71,880
H. Indirect Costs * 65% of S&W (subtotal A) predetermined HHS	$19,500	$13,650	$33,150
I. TOTAL COSTS	$63,728	$41,402	$105,030
COST SHARING = to 39% of I		$41,402	
TOTAL REQUESTED OF AGENCY	$63,728		

*If your rate is based on total direct costs, simply substitute your rate x totals in line G.

Appendix

At the top of our list of items to be included in the Appendix is a description of the institution. The Introduction undoubtedly contains an abbreviated description, such as "_____ College, located in the state of _____, offers a four-year program leading to a B.A. degree to approximately 700 women selected from the fifty states and several foreign countries." A more extensive statement, covering about one page and providing additional descriptive material, belongs in the Appendix. This statement should contain solid, demonstrable facts, e.g. , "The Susan and Emma Cash Library contains 400,000 volumes and subscribes to 900 periodicals." Nebulous or extravagant claims, such as those that often appear in catalogue statements or in promotional brochures, are out of place in this description.

The Appendix should also contain other relevant documentary material that, owing to subject matter, length, or format, would be inappropriate or would disturb the continuity of the narrative. The *curriculum vitae* should definitely be in the Appendix unless otherwise specified. Required letters of endorsement, such as those from cooperating agencies, may be put in the Appendix, unless you are instructed to place them elsewhere. Other documentary material might well include maps, graphs, charts, detailed listings, reports of consultants, special studies related to the project, reading lists, and bibliographies. A decision as to which of these items belong in the body of the proposal and which in the Appendix should be made after you have examined the final draft.

One of the most useful appendices we have seen contained, in proper sequence, some chart, graph, or fact sheets to reinforce or illustrate each major point in the proposal. The appendix thus became a coherent map of the material described in the body of the proposal.

TESTS FOR SOUNDNESS OF A PROPOSAL

General

An underlying, secondary theme in our philosophy of idea development is the importance of evaluative procedures. One of the values inherent in the method described in this guidebook is the almost automatic presence of evaluation from start to finish. The first time an idea is shared, it is evaluated by the second party. From conception to fruition, the idea is exposed to the judgment of others, and the reactions of this constant evaluation foster the idea's growth and development.

In the proposal itself the details of this continuous or "formative" evaluation should be described as background, as evidence of your sound planning process to date, and as an integral part of the procedures of your project. Projects, once started, seldom proceed exactly according to expectations and therefore a plan for constant, continuous assessment should be outlined. Such a plan, devised in the expectation of change, permits change at the most propitious juncture. Anticipation of the circumstances that would lead to change is almost impossible; an assistant with special abilities may have to leave the project, new developments in the field may obviate the need for some of your preparatory work, the sequences of stages in a training program may need amending because the trainees advance faster than expected. A program of continuous evaluation will result in speedy, effective, and often advantageous adjustment to unexpected contingencies.

The process of "summative evaluation" follows the completion of the project. What devices or instruments will be used, what will be done with the results, who will assist, to what extent have objectives been satisfied? It is not sufficient to say, "Outside consultants will be retained with expertise in the field of Training Programs for Women to conduct an impartial evaluation." Such generalities are inadequate for internal planning, as well as for proposals.

Referring back to our example, Improving Competency of Women in Securing Support for Research, there is an obvious built-in device for evaluating this project. First, the sample proposal already suggests a peer review of the trainees' work as the course proceeds. Instructors, reacting to these reviews, can increase the emphasis on certain points that aren't getting across to the trainees. Second, receiving the help of an outside group of reviewers who can judge the trainees' work objectively will ensure a measure of success for the programs. There is at this time no way to measure trainees' improvement in proposal writing since, presumably, they have never before attempted such an exercise. It would be necessary to plan a review of proposals prepared at future times and compare them with the first efforts made in the workshop to determine the effectiveness of the workshop in training participants. Such a review would show not only the extent of continuing interest and motivation but improvements, if any, in the facility of preparing proposals and in the quality of the proposals.

In fact, the idea of writing this guide was precipitated by the expressed interest of the Virginia State Agency for Title I, HEA, Continuing Education and Community Service, in improving the quality of evaluation.

Review Process Criteria

Criteria used by representative funding agencies in judging proposals, together with the processes used in applying the criteria, screening proposals, and reaching decisions appear in Exhibits 9-13. (We have cited several examples, but we call your attention to Exhibits 9 and 10 not because the criteria differ greatly from those used elsewhere, but because they are simply stated and can be easily applied to a variety of proposals.) This sphere of activity is obviously external to the institution and beyond its control. This is not to say, however, that the common criteria and processes of selection are not relevant to the preparation of a proposal. The constant revision of drafts of a proposal results from constant criticism and evaluation on the part of all concerned with the project. An effective way for these internal evaluators to view the proposal objectively is to apply the criteria and simulate the process used by external evaluators.

Among funding agencies there is more variety in the mechanics of selection than in the criteria for selection. The process of selection reflects the size of the funding agency or organization, its goals, the amount of money it has to disburse, the annual volume of proposals received, and whether it is tax-supported or privately supported. The decision-making process may be the responsibility of a permanent board, large or small, whose membership represents broad, general backgrounds or very limited, specialized fields. The decision makers, on the other hand, may be groups of peers in your own field invited to serve on a panel for the express purpose of screening. The so-called peer panel is an example of the latter, where members of the panel are specialists in the field represented by a collection of proposals; the panel meets in one place at one time, each member rates each proposal, and the final decision rests on this collective rating. A peer panel may also discuss the most promising proposals before reaching a decision. A proposal may also be mailed to selected peers for their independent reviews, and their ratings are then assessed by the agency.

In preparing a particular proposal, when a decision has been made on which agencies might be interested in it, it is not out of order—in fact it is advisable—to correspond with or visit the agencies. The agency, after all, has the responsibility of investing money in the wisest ways consistent with its stated goals. A representative of the agency thus often welcomes the opportunity to discuss a preliminary proposal or abstract with a representative of the institution, to describe the agency's goals and standards of selection, and to explain ways in which the proposal does or does not meet the particular requirements and criteria of the agency. This representative frequently encourages the proposal writer to rewrite a proposal, and often will make an estimate of the revised document's chances of receiving a grant.

One of the most successful devices for assessing the quality of a proposal is to present it to a group of your colleagues who will judge it by criteria used by the federal government, or in terms of the standards of the particular foundation to which it will be submitted. A group of eight or ten faculty members representing a variety of disciplines, some of whom have experience in presentation and review of proposals, can be asked to serve as internal reviewers. The flaws, vaguenesses, and presumptions will be found. Final revisions would then be made on the basis of the collective judgment of this group, and individual criticisms and suggestions of the members. This exercise of internal review is educational, and time spent in performing it is worthwhile in improving the quality of proposals. The following pages give samples of the kinds of guidelines given to reviewers. Read these various requirements for review and the questions that must be answered. The order and the wording of the forms may vary but the questions do not.

Ask several of your colleagues to apply the Department of Education's review questions to your proposal. Would they reject it? Fund it? Or suggest changes to clarify and strengthen it?

Following the samples of review criteria is a list of shortcomings in proposals to the National Institutes of Health. The problems with weak proposals haven't changed since these data were compiled.

Exhibit 9. A Private Foundation's (Bank's) Helpful Hints for Proposal Reviewers.

HELPFUL HINTS IN ANALYZING A PROPOSAL			
ELEMENTS TO CONSIDER	QUESTIONS TO ASK	IN-HOUSE KNOWLEDGE	OUTSIDE KNOWLEDGE
NEED	Who is assessing the need? Comparative figures Is program really charitable? (IRS tax-determination imperative; make sure proposal meets WCT guidelines)	Minority employment served Training needs Geographic area (branch banks) Customer relationships	Metropolitan Cultural Alliance United Community Planning Council Associated Foundation of Greater Boston Governmental Agencies Other Foundations (Permanent Charities)
OBJECTIVES	Is there a goal? What is it? Is it realistic?	Experience with other similar proposals Experience in bank with similar objectives (training, recruiting, etc.)	
PROGRAM	Has it been tried before? What was the result? What specific methods are being used to take advantage of other resources?	What other similar programs is bank involved in? (direct or indirect, i.e., United Way)	
BUDGET	(In reviewing the proposal budget, we should carefully screen to see if sound accounting practices are employed)		
MANAGEMENT	What is the role of the organization's Board of Directors? Is group visable (i.e., do they supervise policy--check internal operation, etc.)? How are staff and clients recruited? Does staff member have job definition? Are local people in neighborhood employed? Do they have adequate insurance, licensing, etc?	Experience with corporate or Bank staff serving on organization's Board of Directors Compare B and C with Bank experience	
BUILDING	(Refer to Organization's Guideline)	Use Bank/Management expertise in evaluation process (i.e., is this a good investment?)	
EVALUATION	Criteria for evaluations should be pre-established What is being measured? Is progress being made? On-site visits Reports from Organizations		
FUNDING	Where is funding coming from? Is funding objective realistic? Is it capital vs. operating funds? Will funds be needed for continuation of project in future years (i.e., will new facility create greater future budget needs)?	What are alternatives to assisting project vs. direct financial aid Examples: A. MeCA-Bank matching contributions/ memberships B. Loan vs. Grant C. Volunteer activity-staff help	AFGB computer list re current funding to similar organizations Is this funded through United Way? Are other corporations supporting this project? Local contracts, "Givers' Groups" support?

Exhibit 10. The U.S. Department of Education's Criteria for Evaluation Provided to Reviewers.

EVALUATION CRITERIA	YES	NO	COMMENTS	WEIGHT FACTOR
MANAGEMENT--Identify the applicant's organizational elements, and describe how they function internally, including subcontracts, to insure the project is accomplished within the time limits and resources available.				
1. Is the proposed plan of operation sound? Consideration of soundness should include the following points: Are the objects of the project capable of being attained by the proposed procedures and capable of being measured?				
Are provisions made for adequate evaluation of the effectiveness of the project and for determining the extent to which the objectives are accomplished?				
Where appropriate, are provisions made for satisfactory inservice training connected with project services? and,				
Are provisions made for disseminating the results of the project and for making materials, techniques, and other output resulting therefrom, available to the general public and specifically to all those concerned with the area of education with which the project is itself concerned?				
2. Published Application Review Criteria				
FINANCE & ACCOUNTING --Provide adequate project cost details to support the proposed budget in relation to the anticipated end results.				
1. Is the estimated cost reasonable to the anticipated results?				
COMMENTS: (use extra sheets)				

EVALUATION CRITERIA	YES	NO	COMMENTS	WEIGHT FACTOR
ORGANIZATION--Describe the applicant's background, facilities and personnel expertise as it relates to performing the proposed project. 1. Are the qualifications and experience of applicant's personnel adequate to carry out the proposed project?				
2. Are applicant's facilities and other resources adequate?				
3. Published Application Review Criteria				
PROGRAMMATIC--Define all the work and related resources required to perform the applicant's proposed project pursuant to the applicable regulations. 1. Is the proposed activity needed in the area served or to be served by the applicant?				
2. Is the proposal relevant to priority areas of concern as reflected in provisions contained in the applicable Federal statutes and regulations?				
3. Is there potential for utilizing the results of the proposed project in other projects or programs for similar educational purposes?				
4. Are the size, scope and duration of the project sufficient in order to secure productive results?				
5. Are the objectives of the proposed project sharply defined and clearly stated?				
6. Published Application Review Criteria				
COMMENTS: (use extra sheets)				

Exhibit 11. A Foundation Official's Advice for Reviewing a Proposal Budget.

REVIEWING A PROPOSAL'S BUDGET

The proposal should provide:

1. A projected income and expense statement for the year for which funding is being sought, as well as a statement of actual income and expenses for the previous year.

2. If the request is for a special program or capital project, budgets for the program or project should be included in addition to the agency's overall budget.

3. The income statement should itemize by category amounts received from:

   fees
   donations
   fund-raising events
   government contracts or grants
   United Way allocations
   foundation grants
   individual contributions
   other

4. The expense statement should itemize expenditures within the the following categories:

   salaries
   fringe benefits
   social security
   rent
   utilities
   materials and supplies
   other (consultant fees, transportation costs, etc.)
   equipment needs

5. Provide an audited financial statement if available.

Exhibit 12. A Corporate Foundation's Proposal Review Sheet.

```
                    A CORPORATION'S REVIEW SHEET

                        Proposal Review

ORGANIZATION_____

      FOUNDATION_____TURNDOWN_____DATE OF REVIEW_____

1.    Quick evaluation of purpose and amount requested:_____

      _____

      _____

      _____

      _____

      _____

      _____

      Total Budget_____Area to be served_____

      Project  Administrator_____

      Business Address_____

      Indication of ability to raise funds from other sources for this

      purpose:_____

      _____

2.    Amount, Date and purpose of previous grants:  _____

      _____

      _____

      Acknowledgement Card_____Date_____Additional Comments_____

      _____

      _____

      on file  requested                    on file  requested
      _____  _____  IRS Letter        _____  _____  Income statement
      _____  _____  Budget per        _____  _____  Audited report
                          req. purpose      _____  _____  Staff background
      _____  _____  Overall budgt     _____  _____  Board list
```

Exhibit 13. A List of Shortcomings from the National Institutes of Health.

NATIONAL INSTITUTES OF HEALTH

SHORTCOMINGS FOUND IN STUDY-SECTION* REVIEW OF 605 DISAPPROVED
RESEARCH GRANT APPLICATIONS

No.	Shortcoming

Class I: Problem

1. The problem is of insufficient importance or is unlikely to produce any new or useful information.

2. The proposed research is based on a hypothesis that rests on insufficient evidence, is doubtful, or is unsound.

3. The problem is more complex than the investigator appears to realize.

4. The problem has only local significance, or is one of production or control, or otherwise fails to fall sufficiently clearly within the general field of health-related research.

5. The problem is scientifically premature and warrants, at most, only a pilot study.

6. The research as proposed is overly involved, with too many elements under simultaneous investigation.

7. The description of the nature of the research and of its significance leave the proposal nebulous and diffuse and without clear research aim.

Class II: Approach

8. The proposed tests, or methods, or scientific procedures are unsuited to the stated objectives.

9. The description of the approach is too nebulous, diffuse, and lacking in clarity to permit adequate evaluation.

10. The overall design of the study has not been carefully thought out.

11. The statistical aspects of the approach have not been given sufficient consideration.

12. The approach lacks scientific imagination.

13. Controls are either inadequately conceived or inadequately described.

14. The material the investigator proposes to use is unsuited to the objectives of the study or is difficult to obtain.

15. The number of observations is unsuitable.

16. The equipment contemplated is outmoded or otherwise unsuitable.

NATIONAL INSTITUTES OF HEALTH

No.	Shortcoming

Class III: Personnel

17. The investigator does not have adequate experience or training, or both, for this research

18. The investigator appears to be unfamiliar with pertinent literature or methods, or both.

19. The investigator's previously published work in this field does not inspire confidence.

20. The investigator proposes to rely too heavily on insufficiently experienced associates.

21. The investigator is spreading himself too thin; he will be more productive if he concentrates on fewer projects.

22. The investigator needs more liaison with colleagues in this field or in collateral fields.

Class IV: Other

23. The requirements for equipment or personnel, or both are unrealistic.

24. It appears that other responsibilities would prevent devotion of sufficient time and attention to the research.

25. The institutional setting is unfavorable.

26. Research grants to the investigator, now in force, are adequate in scope and amount to cover the proposed research.

---

* Study-sections are advisory boards organized according to fields of study and composed of research scientists nationwide.

Finding a Source for Support

Go first to the institution's Grants Officer. If there is no Grants Officer or Office of Development, go to the head of the institution to make sure that certain sources of funds are not already being approached to support other institutional programs. Never, under any circumstances, approach an outside agency without clearance from the Development or Grants Office or the head of the institution; such independent action could not only jeopardize an institution's prior request but often results in neither request being granted because the credibility of the institution appears in a dubious light to the agency. Most individuals in an institution are ignorant of the various institutional projects contemplated and the kind of orchestration that must be devised by those responsible for setting institutional priorities in seeking supporting funds.

Assuming advice in this guide has been followed, the Originator has already described the idea, project, and dimensions of the project to the Grants Officer. This officer or his or her deputy has readily at hand the Catalogue of Federal Domestic Assistance and many other source materials to aid the Originator in selecting potential sources of funds. Together they will prepare a list of prospects, but the major responsibility for this task belongs, naturally, to the Grants Officer. Experienced and capable Grants Officers do their homework thoroughly before a final list is compiled, certainly before any funding agency is approached. The officer will first study the stated purpose and recent grants record of each prospective source of funds and will eliminate those not compatible with the project under consideration. Suppose, for instance, a foundation is interested in problems of the aging. What sort of work does it favor in attacking these problems? Basic research? Teacher training? Direct services in the areas of health, continuing education, etc.? Much time will be saved if the prospective donor's objectives are thoroughly understood. This understanding also indicates to the donor the degree of accountability and seriousness of purpose of the applicant. If some funding sources fail to state what they will support, write and ask for their guidelines. These tasks ultimately yield a final list of potential donors.

The next step for the Originator and Grants Officer is to prepare a letter of inquiry and a description of the plan to send to each agency on the final list. It is essential, whether dealing with donors in person or in writing, that the Originator and Grants Officer work together. The latter brings experience to the job, but this experience without full understanding of the project may produce a presentation which at best is superficial, at worst phony. Integrity and understanding of the project must mark the initial and all later contacts with donors, and these qualities can be achieved only if the Originator and Grants Officer work together.

Considerable advice is available on methods of approaching prospective donors, but in the end sensitivity, good judgment, and luck may play equal parts in winning their confidence. An experienced Grants Officer already has a fairly good idea of how to approach various private sources. How important, for instance, is direct contact through a member of the institution's Board of Trustees or some other friend of the institution? Should an interview be requested and, if so, who should make the call? The Grants Officer? The Originator? The Board Member? The President? Or some combination of these individuals? There is no one answer to these questions except to do what the foundation or corporation tells applicants to do. Some welcome a personal call, some suffer it, and some refuse to discuss a plan until it is deemed appropriate to their own interests on the basis of a written abstract or draft. An influential trustee with contacts on a foundation's board may reinforce a statement of competency and open doors for the applicant, but the more professional the staff of a foundation the less valuable knowing the right person will be. Experience proves, of course, that some foundations make decisions on a personal basis, but, in general, the best advice to applicants is to place their trust in the quality of their effort and the professionalism of the foundation, not in personal contacts.

Follow the same advice when you apply to a government agency, except that you can assume that every grant program has a professional staff. Whatever you have heard of using congressional help in securing favorable action on a proposal, our best advice is to inform your senators and representatives of your intentions but do not ask them to exert influence on your behalf. An even better procedure would be for the official in your organization responsible for government relations to inform the representatives and for them to make the decision as to just what should be reported and how. There are a few instances where congressional intercession has helped, but more instances where such intrusion has so antagonized the agency staff that its forced approval of a project may be its last positive response to your proposals. Agency tenure tends to outlast congressional tenure.

The same planning and attention to details should mark the applicant's approach to foundations as has marked other parts of the process of growth and development of an idea. Follow the advice and instruction of each of the foundations on the final list. An abstract of twenty pages may be acceptable to one, five pages to another, one page to still another. The preparation of each is an exercise in combining degrees of brevity and precision while preserving the chief ideas and information needed by the donors.

Government programs may have very sharply focused interests, such as those described in the guidelines of the National Science Foundation's Research in Undergraduate Institutions Program or the Department of Education's Cooperative Education Program. Secure guidelines from these agencies and be sure that the application follows all directions regarding content, format, and order. Remember that an agency's guidelines not only reflect the many voices which aided in their preparation but also have had to be cleared by the agency's legal counsel, finance officers, and legislative liaison officer, and in final form may seem to contain ambiguities. It is strongly recommended that you visit or at least make a phone call to the agency's Program Officer before submitting a proposal or preliminary proposal, to discover whether you have correctly interpreted all directions.

Most of the preceding advice is based on the assumption that the institution provides competent professional help in finding outside support; details have been included, however, that will make the advice equally or even more

useful to those lacking such help. The following additional tips will help those in such a situation. Most large city libraries carry the *Federal Register* along with other publications. Headquarters of the United Way and other large charitable institutions or development offices of colleges and universities subscribe to and hold many publications of sources. The Foundation Library has many branches and its staff is notably competent and helpful. The phone book lists local foundations and these usually have the *Foundation Directory. The Directory of Research Grants,* describing nearly 6,000 research funding sources, may also be helpful. You may wish to purchase or subscribe to some of the basic sources of general information to become familiar with the kinds of sources and the level of sophistication grant seeking has reached. In short, do the homework and give no less attention to answering the questions and following the specifications of a funding source than to other phases of guiding a developing project to completion.

To clarify the viewpoint of the prospective supporter or donor we quote part of a paper given by Nils Y. Wessell, former president of the Alfred P. Sloan Foundation. The full text of his paper appeared in the *Society of Research Administrators Journal,* Spring 1975. The comments apply to his foundation's position and probably reflect the position of an increasing number of foundations.

> I could not believe my eyes and ears one bright morning when the three individuals who represented my ten o'clock appointment walked in carrying an easel and colored flipcharts. One of the three served only as a flipper of the charts on cue. The second must have been a former Florida underwater land salesman. The third was the president of the institution who simply sat in the background, grinned, and nodded his head. The faculty members who conceived the project and were to carry it out, given support, and who were the only ones who really understood what it was all about, were hundreds of miles away back home. That is what I call the Madison Avenue brand of sophistication. Making the whole thing even more unbelievable was the fact that if any one of them had bothered to read our last annual report, he would have known that the proposed program was specifically one which did not meet our program guidelines.

Don't start your funding search with a "ceremonial" visit. Do your homework to learn what the funding source is interested in or how it wishes to be approached.

Submission of a Proposal

Although every agency or funding source has its own peculiar requirements that should be met to the letter, it is safe to say that the total body of material, ready to be submitted for consideration, will consist of (1) a cover sheet; (2) letters of endorsement; and (3) the proposal proper, in exactly this order. This material represents everything you wish to have considered by a reviewer. These pages should be secured by a single staple or grommet in the upper lefthand corner. Do not add protective or decorative covers and bindings, for these will be promptly torn off to expose the official cover sheet as well as to lighten the load and to facilitate filing. A letter of transmittal should accompany the proposal but should not be permanently attached to it.

The contents of the proposal have already been described in the section on parts of a proposal, but more should be said concerning the cover sheet and letters of endorsement and transmittal; the latter are briefly referred to in the section on parts of a proposal.

COVER SHEET

The cover sheet is always the top page and carries all of the information that identifies your organization and proposal. Federal agencies usually provide their own forms for a cover sheet; the forms vary from program to program but the same kinds of data are sought and probably include:

Employer Identification Number (E.I.N.), which is the same number assigned to an employer in connection with Federal Withholding Tax.

State Clearing House Number. Certain programs require clearance with the State Planning Commission before action can be taken on a proposal. In other cases state institutions must secure clearance from the planning authorities and their state education commissions. This matter is under study by the federal government and changes in regulations and requirements can be expected. The agency you are applying to can tell you whether its program requires state clearance. Your regional office, state commission on education, or state planning commission can provide you with the needed information and appropriate forms to file.

These may seem trivial points, but you can be ruled out on technicalities such as omission of pieces of required information.

Cover sheets or your own title page should also contain certain other information:
1. The title of the project
2. Name and address of institution
3. Project Director's name, address, and telephone number
4. Dollar amount of grant requested
5. Signature of authorizing official at your institution, usually the president
6. Chief Fiscal Officer's name, title, address, and telephone number; Grants Officer's name, title, address, and telephone number
7. Proposed date for starting project
8. Submission date

LETTERS OF ENDORSEMENT

Letters of endorsement, if you wish reviewers to read them, follow the cover sheet or may be placed in the Appendix. The letter of transmittal accompanies the proposal but is not permanently attached to it and is presumably filed separately by the official to whom it is addressed. A letter of endorsement signed by the officer empowered to speak for your institution is an appropriate or even very desirable part of your proposal because it assures the reviewer of the institution's confidence in and commitment to your project. In the case of a cooperative venture, the endorsement of each of the heads of the cooperating institutions should be included. The letter of endorsement should contain (a) a brief statement endorsing the idea of the proposal, (b) an explanation of why the particular agency was selected (i.e., the philosophy and objectives expressed in its literature and policy statement make it appropriate for the envisioned project), and (c) a request that the accompanying request for _____ to support the project over a period of _____ years be given serious consideration.

The letter of endorsement may also contain other points that the signer believes will reinforce the potential significance of the project to the institution.

LETTER OF TRANSMITTAL

Every proposal to a private funding source should be accompanied by a transmittal letter. State which program you are applying to, what sum of money you need, and what you want the reader of your letter to do, i.e., do you want that person to read it, file it, or respond to it?

It is wise to enclose a letter of transmittal with your proposal even though a letter of endorsement is already an inclusion. The letter of transmittal, signed by the person authorized to speak for the institution, asks the receiver to do whatever is necessary to have your proposal considered. This letter may be all that is required as an endorsement, or the letter of endorsement may be an exact copy of the letter of transmittal. (See Exhibit 14.)

TYPING REQUIREMENTS

Note the typing requirements, if any. If there are few or no specifications we suggest the following:

1. Use blank white 8½ x 11 paper
2. Set your word processing program to use a standard type face no smaller than 12 point, double-space between lines, and leave a 1½ inch margin on the sides and bottom, a 1 inch margin at the top
3. Place page numbers at top right corner, center top or bottom, but be consistent
4. Put the organization's or Project Director's name at lower left corner of each page or block of pages that might be extracted from the full proposal for purposes of handling and circulation, e.g., cover sheet, budget page, abstract, vita
5. Use capital letters for main headings, subheadings in upper and lower case letters
6. Consider the advantages of outlining your proposal, using a conventional system of numbers and letters to designate sections and subsections; some word processing programs have outline formats
7. Beside each budget item note the page where this item is described in the narrative portion of your proposal.
8. Provide a table of contents; include the page number where each section or subsection begins; provide appropriate outline numbers and letters if this system has been used in your proposal.
9. Be sure that section headings and subheadings and outline designations in the table of contents correspond exactly to those in the body of the proposal,

Exhibit 14. Example Letter of Transmittal.

_____, 19____

Dr. William Black, Executive Director
The Susan and Emma Cash Foundation
1000 East Bay Street
Boston, MA 02101
Dear Dr. Black: (title)

The enclosed proposal _____ has been addressed to the Susan and Emma Cash Foundation in response to your stated interest in projects that will improve the ability of women to compete in professional activities. We have noted that your upper limit of support for administration training programs is $50,000. Our proposed training program will require $31,280 for implementation.

I am personally familiar with the thorough study and detailed plans that Professor Edna Driver has carried out to prepare this proposal. Since _____ College is committed to the education of women and has a faculty with an excellent record in research and project design we heartily endorse this project as an appropriate mission for this institution. Should you have any further questions concerning the institution's commitment or Professor Driver's plan, please feel free to call me or to call Professor Driver directly.

Sincerely yours,

(signed)

Title: President; Executive Director, etc.

and that all references to these items correspond similarly.

10. Some agencies specify margins and type size; follow their instructions

FINALLY AND FIRST: FOLLOW INSTRUCTIONS, FOLLOW INSTRUCTIONS

1. Check to be certain of the deadline:

   Date for receipt of proposal; or

   Date for mailing (send by Certified Mail to ensure safety, and also to guarantee having evidence of date of sending, keep the receipt, Express Mail and commercial carriers' receipts are not always acceptable proof to the agency) or;

   Date for hand-delivery.

2. Do not ask for extensions unless there is some real and urgent reason. Do not expect to receive an extension.

THE FINAL CHECK

Before submission, make one final check. Have you included:

1. Required assurances and certification—for example, Civil Rights Act, Treatment of Human Subjects, Animal Subjects, Drug-Free Work Place, Lobbying, Debarment and Suspension, etc. (See forms and regulations in Basic Resources, Section IV, page 118.)
2. Correct number of copies, including extras of any section requested?
3. Internal Revenue statement on tax-exempt and private foundation status?
4. A *curriculum vitae* for the Project Director and each person with a key post in the project?
5. All official forms filled out as per instructions of the funding agency?
6. Required signatures of officials in your institution?

Submit your proposal and patiently wait for a response from the funding agency.

Grant Administration

Accountability and capacity to account for funds and the activities in a funded project are increasingly considerations in making a grant. Your track record in doing what you proposed as supported by sound evaluative practice and good fiscal accounting puts you in a stronger position for future grants. The following pages provide an administrative process designed to accommodate small organizations and institutions where there may be only one or two people responsible for management of grant funds.

First we will go through some of the typical responses you might receive from a sponsor and how to respond.

We then provide some general advice and checklists to prepare you for securing and spending awarded funds.

Following that general advice is a section to help you negotiate an agreement if you are not offered full funding for your project.

Next we offer suggestions for action if your proposal is rejected.

Finally we will lead you through the process starting with a sample budget, typical communication with the grantor, award letters, forms for justifying and authorizing payments, and a simple spread sheet for record keeping.

COMMUNICATION FROM AND WITH THE SPONSOR

The day eventually comes when you hear from the outside agency whose support you sought for your project. Below are the kinds of replies you may receive and some of the possible ensuing actions you can take:

1. A form or personalized letter rejecting your proposal; respond politely and ask for more explicit comments as to why you were turned down. Explain that you would value constructive criticism to guide you in considering resubmission;

2. Request for additional information. Provide what is requested promptly;

3. Letter suggesting that you (a) review your proposal, (b) limit your project activities, or (c) decrease the dollar amount of your request. A conference should be sought: following such a meeting revise your proposal if this can be done without jeopardizing your mission or the quality of the anticipated results;

4. Official letter stating that a grant or contract is going to be awarded to you. Some agencies require an official acceptance signed by (a) the official authorized to obligate the institution and (b) the Project Director. Others assume you have accepted unless you tell them otherwise. If your grant comes from a federal agency your congressional representative is always notified first. The good news thus usually comes from your elected representative.

PREPARATION FOR SECURING AND EXPENDING THE GRANT FUNDS

Don't count on spending the first dollar until you have the funds in hand. Before you arrange to draw down the funds from the grantor (the federal government usually makes payments upon submission of quarterly request vouchers while some private foundations will remit the entire grant amount in one check in advance) we suggest the following preparation:

1. Discuss your grant and the institution's procedures for handling grant funds with the Fiscal Officer. Learn what steps you must follow to secure payment of expenses. We assume some person, probably the Grants or Sponsored Programs Officer again, is responsible for overseeing the official accounting for grants and contracts. You should learn from that person and the agency what latitude you have in spending funds without seeking a "change order" from the grantor, and what kinds of expenditures are not allowed. Re-read your agency guidelines and your proposal with care.

2. Keep complete records for yourself as a double check to those of your grant administrator. It is wise to assume there will be an audit and, thus, to maintain not only official records but work paper to refresh your memory after the work has been completed. All correspondence with the grantor and a record of all expenditures should be kept in the files so that you can tell what has been spent and what funds remain at any given time.

3. For the purposes of making payments on grant activities a special voucher form is recommended that has spaces for the internal account number, the grant number, the grantor or agency, identification of expenditure by line item, the Project Director's signature, and the signature of that person in the business office who authorizes payments.

The following is a summary checklist to assist you in anticipating and solving the major administrative problems:

- Acknowledge the award and secure the grantor's guide or requirements for accounting and reporting.

- Meet with your Fiscal Officer and have an account established for your grant so that it will be included in the regular accounting of the institution.

- Learn what you should do to secure payments from the grant.

- Prepare an estimate of your expected costs for the next three months, and ask the Fiscal Office to request these funds from the grantor (assuming the money has not been paid in advance).

- Advise all participants to discuss their expected expenses with you and review all expected costs before spending the money.

- If expenses are at variance with those projected in the original proposal, revise your budget accordingly and secure permission to make the changes if such permission is required by the grantor. Usually there is a limit on changes allowed without permission. Permission is usually required for additions or deletions of line items.

- All requests for expenditures should be approved by the Project Director and forwarded to the Fiscal Office for review and payment.

- File copies of all vouchers submitted for payment.

- Statements of services performed should be made or appended to vouchers. The name, time spent, and budget items authorizing the activity should be on the voucher.

- Request for travel reimbursement must be accompanied by airline stubs, hotel bills, and other receipts as required by your institutional policy.

- In arranging compensation for temporary personnel, work with the Fiscal Officer to be certain that Social Security and benefits are covered. The round figure in the proposal budget should cover all costs, not just the gross salary.

- Be alert to requirements for competitive bids or acceptable justification for dealing with a particular supplier.

- All extra compensation for regular employees of an institution is subject to Social Security and income tax withholding based on the employee's total compensation from that institution.

- Certain grants for study made to particular individuals are considered fellowships and are not subject to income tax. The awarding agency should be consulted to determine the classification. However the IRS Code makes it clear that the term fellowship is not synonymous with "tax exempt." Most work under grants and contracts is treated as taxable income.

- Most federal grants set a limit of $250 per day plus expenses for fees for consultants. Find out what the current rate is and be certain of your authority before paying consultant fees.

- Foreign travel, although approved as a line item in a grant budget, must have specific approval from the federal agency involved before the trip is taken.

- Prepare and file your required reports on time.

NEGOTIATION AND ACCEPTANCE

Your award letter or a telephone call from the sponsor has come. Ideally they will say they desire to provide assistance in the amount you requested in the proposal. If this is the case, there is little problem and your most important task is to review any accompanying terms, conditions, or stipulations to be sure:

1. your institution is prepared to comply and
2. the terms conform to the policies and practices of your institution

For example, if the project involves human subjects, there are federal regulations covering their use and treatment. Or, the sponsor may request certain restrictions on publishing material derived from the project. You should make sure that any such restrictions are in concert with your own institutional policies before accepting the award.

Unfortunately, total funding of the amount requested in your proposal is a rare occurrence. Usually you will receive a letter or telephone call suggesting that you revise your proposal by:

- limiting your project activity or
- decreasing the dollar amount of your request

It is important at this point to review the sponsor's request with the Grants Officer as that person usually accepts the award on behalf of the institution and is therefore familiar with institutional policy and negotiations. The Project Director and Grants Officer, either by letter or telephone, must seek a resolution with the sponsor. When a general agreement is reached, prepare a revised proposal that does not jeopardize the mission of the project or quality of the anticipated results. The next step is usually the receipt of an official award letter stating a grant or contract has been awarded to your institution to perform the project you proposed. Some agencies require official acceptance signed by the person authorized to obligate the institution. Others will assume that you accept the award unless you tell them otherwise. You are now at liberty to begin work and expect the sponsor to pay for the costs.

REJECTION/SELF-APPRAISAL/ RESUBMISSION

If the communication you receive from the outside agency is a form or personalized letter rejecting your proposal, do not despair.

The competition for funding of academic and other proposals for research and/or curriculum and instruction programs is very keen. In fact, the number of requests for funding from federal and foundation sources has shown a significant increase over the past decade. The rejection of a proposal for funding is a common occurrence— particularly in the case of a first submission.

One of the most important steps to be taken after a rejection is to learn why the submission was unsuccessful. All federal agencies are obligated to provide you with either a written or oral debriefing on the reasons for the denial. In the case of federal agencies, which use "peer review" or "study-section review" in proposal evaluations, copies of the reviews are available to the Project

Director upon request. You should always request the written evaluation or an oral debriefing.

The situation for unsuccessful foundation proposals is quite different. There is no obligation to furnish the grant applicant with any reasons for denial. Nevertheless, one should always pursue any agency directly or indirectly as to the reasons for rejection. Some foundations will not provide any information. Still others are very helpful and constructive in discussing the rejection. It is generally a good idea to conduct a self-appraisal to complement the sponsor's comments on denial by asking questions of the following nature:

1. How pressing a need does the project fill?
2. Does the proposal demonstrate a clear anticipation of problems that are likely to occur, and an awareness of relevant scholarship and available resources?
3. How does the applicant's background (education, publications, professional standing) clearly qualify him or her to carry out this project successfully?
4. Is the budget sound?
5. In general, does the proposal have promise of making a significant contribution?

For the self-appraisal to be worthwhile, one must be objective and brutally frank.

The only purpose of the internal critique and solicitation of the reasons the proposal was not funded is to secure information to guide you in considering resubmission. Through the information you have gathered, there should be strong possibilities of improving the quality of the blueprint for carrying out your ideas.

Don't get discouraged by rejection. Consider and weigh the reviewers' comments and strengthen your proposal for resubmission. The chances of funding are much greater for proposals that have been improved and resubmitted.

A CASE STUDY FOR ADMINISTRATION OF A GRANT

Anyville College Receives an Award

Anyville College has submitted a proposal to the Department of Education to develop a new program in Latin American Studies. Faculty need released time during the academic year to participate in a course developed over the summer. A consultant will be brought in to meet with faculty during their summer working sessions for assistance with evaluation after courses are tested. The narrative description of costs is a reflection of the detailed description of activities in the narrative. The original budget submitted requested $42,000. Five thousand was for part-time secretarial support. Seven months have passed since the submission deadline. The person listed on the cover sheet of the proposal in section 4, contact person, receives a phone call from a person in the agency grants/contracts office to discuss some budget changes. The Grants or Sponsored Program Officer's name is not on the cover sheet, just the Project Director' name: In this case study Jane Doe is the Project Director and since there is no place for the Grants Officers' name on the cover sheet, Jane Doe receives the phone call from the Education Department to discuss the budget. Anne Perking is the Education Department contact specialist. Ms. Perking asks Jane Doe to reduce her submitted budget by $5000, and eliminate the secretary since Anyville's overhead includes secretarial support. Professor Doe recognizes that she does not have authority to make a change of this sort without consulting with the Anyville Grants Officer, George Smith. George Smith calls Ms. Perking and agrees to the reduction in the budget. Ms. Perking asks for a revised "budget" to be submitted in one week, revising the new grant total to $37,000. In addition to the reduction, Ms. Perking asks the Grants Officer, George Smith, for an explanation of the basis for Professor Rich's salary and for assurance that the college will support his released time.

The Cast of People Involved

Before we move on to the example budgets, letters, and forms, let us list below the cast of people involved in the awarding and administering of this grant.

First Actions to Be Taken

The first thing to be done is the preparation of a written response to the Education Department's Grants Special-

ist, Ms. Perking. This requires a letter from George Smith answering her questions, and a revised budget and revised coversheet. (See Exhibits 16 and 18–19.) Anyville President Dr. Bartholomew Pressley needs to write a letter to the Program Officer, approving Smith's revised budget (Exhibit 17). This documentation is important for your records. At last an official award letter arrives addressed to the President and/or the Project Director. This letter will be accompanied by an official award document citing the award number, authorized funding, the budget period, the project period, and the method of payment. (See Exhibit 21.) Review this document carefully to be certain it contains the information you agreed too. This document is the official authorization telling you the granted money is available.

Spending the Grant Funds

The following post-award process for administration of sponsored programs (grants) was designed for a small college or organization. It defines a sponsored program for the purpose of determining who is responsible for accounting, approving expenditures, and reporting. It also calls for three signatures on each voucher in order to have a check written. This procedure protects everyone from making unallowable expenditures, incorrect calculations, and overexpenditures of funds. This procedure provides documentation for each expenditure sufficient to meet audit requirements.

Anyville College—Post-Award Policy

All projects funded from external sources—government, foundation, corporation, or individuals—with multiple line item budgets, time limitations for expenditure of grant funds, and/or requirements for fiscal reports are defined as "sponsored programs" and are subject to these procedures for administration of grants.

Exhibit 15. A List of People Involved.

• Anyville Project Director	Jane Doe—It's her proposal and project to carry out
• Pres. of Anyville College	Dr. Bartholomew Pressley—He is the person with authority to commit the resources of Anyville
• Education Department Program Officer	Dr. Edna Green—Government Official for Program Decisions
• Education Department Grants/Contract Specialist	Ms. Anne Perking—Government Official for Fiscal Decisions
• Anyville Sponsored Program Officer	George Smith—College Official for Administration of Grants
• Anyville Business Officer	Susan S. Jones—College Official who issues checks

1. Awards. Notification may come to the President or the Principal Investigator/Project Director (PI/PD).

Upon receipt of notification of award, copies of the award documents or letter should be sent to the Fiscal Officer and the Director of Sponsored Programs. The latter will forward the information to the Dean and the Director of Development.

Any changes in the budget for obligation of time and college facilities must be approved by the person(s) authorized to obligate the college—the President, Chief Fiscal Officer.

When required, an acceptance of the award should be sent to the funding source in accordance with its instructions. The grantor may require an acknowledgment from the President or the Chief Fiscal Officer. The Director of Sponsored Programs must review the award to make certain there are no unexpected terms and conditions in the award documents. (See Exhibit 21.)

2. Administration of Grants—The Anyville College Prior Approval System. The Director of Sponsored Programs has the responsibility for this Organizational Prior Approval System (OPAS) to meet federal requirements.

Have the Fiscal Officer assign an account number to the grant. (See Exhibit 22.) Provide the PI/PD with a supply of vouchers, (see Exhibit 23) time and effort report sheets, and secretarial log sheets.

Maintain expenditure records on an accrual basis. (See Exhibit 24.)

Provide the PI/PD with guidance on allowable changes and assistance in securing approval of modifications.

3. Expenditures (Procedures and Policy Information). PI/PD initiates request for expenditures.

The Director of Sponsored Programs reviews request to see that there are funds in the grant account and that the expenditure is allowable under the grant/contract terms and conditions.

The Fiscal Officer checks the voucher after it is signed by PI/PD and Director of Sponsored Programs and signs to authorize payment.

All vouchers must be supported by internal purchase orders with supplier's invoices, Anyville travel vouchers and documentation, and time and effort reports as appropriate.

Purchase orders must be initiated by the Director of Sponsored Programs to obligate funds. This is important since the monthly expenditure reports provided to the PI/PD are on an accrual basis and federal fiscal reports are made on an accrual basis.

No changes can be made in salary and wage items or items specifically limited by the grantor without prior approval of the Director of Sponsored Programs because these changes may reflect additional costs to the college.

Anyville employment policy applies to all grants and contracts unless prior approval for deviation in policy is approved by the President/Dean/Chief Fiscal Officer.

4. Reports. Final fiscal reports will be prepared by the PI/PD and Sponsored Programs Officer for signature and transmittal by the Chief Fiscal Officer (see Exhibit 25).

PI/PD is responsible for preparing nonfiscal project reports in time to meet the grantor's schedule.

5. General Information. Current fringe benefit and indirect cost rates are available from the Sponsored Programs Officer. The rates are revised annually under a formula set by the government by OMB Ruling A-21.

The Department of Health and Human Services (HHS) is the cognizant agency and has the responsibility for audit of all federal funds. Anyville College is required to conduct an annual audit of federal funds.

Summer salaries for faculty are calculated at 1/9 of the academic year base salary unless some other terms are negotiated and agreed to by the grantee and grantor.

Specific information related to federal regulations for compliance with civil rights, sex and age discrimination, privacy, animal care, safety standards, accessibility for the handicapped, drug-free workplace, and accounting requirements are kept on file. Anyville College policy requires compliance with such regulations.

Department of Education
Contracts Office
7th & D Streets, SW
Washington, DC 20202

Dear Ms. Perking:

Enclosed is a revised budget for Grant #G00000375.

Anyville College will provide the released time required for Professor Rich to serve as the group leader specified on line item A-2. This figure is based on 1/7 base salary per course per term.

The remaining adjustments in the budget reflect actual salaries for Anyville College's next academic year commencing on July 1, 1985, and revised estimates in the other line items based on current costs.

The total of this revised budget is $37,000 from the Department of Education with an additional $15,276 in cost sharing from Anyville College.

I appreciate your assistance in making this revision. Please let me know if you have any further questions.

Sincerely yours,

George Smith
Director Sponsored Programs

GS/prc
Enclosure

Dr. Edna Green
Department of Education
International Studies Branch
7th & D Streets, SW, ROB3
Washington, DC 20202

Dear Dr. Green:

Enclosed is the cover sheet and a revised budget for Grant #G00000375 as requested by your contracting officer. We are pleased to receive this grant to develop and implement a program in Latin American Studies at Anyville College. This revised budget for a total of $37,000 has my approval.

Very truly yours,

Bartholomew Pressley
President

BP/pr
Enclosure

Exhibit 18. Revised Cover Sheet.

OMB Approval No. 29-R0218

FEDERAL ASSISTANCE	2. APPLI-CANT'S APPLI-CATION	a. NUMBER 330.726	3. STATE APPLICA-TION IDENTI-FIER	a. NUMBER
		b. DATE Year month day 19 X1 01 09		b. DATE Year month day ASSIGNED 19

| 1. TYPE OF ACTION (Mark appropriate box) | ☐ PREAPPLICATION ☒ APPLICATION ☐ NOTIFICATION OF INTENT (Opt.) ☐ REPORT OF FEDERAL ACTION | Leave Blank |

4. LEGAL APPLICANT/RECIPIENT

- a. Applicant Name : Anyville College
- b. Organization Unit : Modern Languages
- c. Street/P.O. Box : 0000 South Street
- d. City : Anyville,   e. County : Central
- f. State : E.Va.   g. ZIP Code : 00000
- h. Contact Person (Name & telephone No.) : Dr. Jane Doe 20x-000-0000

5. FEDERAL EMPLOYER IDENTIFICATION NO. 000-000-0000-A1

6. PROGRAM (From Federal Catalog)
- a. NUMBER 8 4 . 0 1 6
- b. TITLE Undergraduate International Studies and Foreign Language Program

7. TITLE AND DESCRIPTION OF APPLICANT'S PROJECT

Latin American Studies: Second year of program designed to bring a Latin American Studies (LAS) program into our International Studies curriculum. Includes: 4 week faculty training, incorporation of material on LA into over 20 existing courses for ca. 300 students a year, teaching an interdisciplinary introductory course on LA.

8. TYPE OF APPLICANT/RECIPIENT
A-State
B-Interstate
C-Substate District
D-County
E-City
F-School District
G-Special Purpose District
H-Community Action Agency
I-Higher Educational Institution
J-Indian Tribe
K-Other (Specify):
Enter appropriate letter [I]

9. TYPE OF ASSISTANCE
A-Basic Grant
B-Supplemental Grant
C-Loan
D-Insurance
E-Other
Enter appropriate letter(s) [A]

10. AREA OF PROJECT IMPACT (Names of cities, counties, States, etc.)
Central County & USA

11. ESTIMATED NUMBER OF PERSONS BENEFITING
250

12. TYPE OF APPLICATION
A-New   C-Revision   E-Augmentation
B-Renewal   D-Continuation
Enter appropriate letter [D]

13. PROPOSED FUNDING		14. CONGRESSIONAL DISTRICTS OF:		15. TYPE OF CHANGE (For 12c or 12e)
a. FEDERAL	$ 37,000 .00	a. APPLICANT 19	b. PROJECT 19	A-Increase Dollars F-Other (Specify):
b. APPLICANT	15,276 .00			B-Decrease Dollars
c. STATE	.00	16. PROJECT START DATE Year month day 19 X1 9 1	17. PROJECT DURATION 12 Months	C-Increase Duration D-Decrease Duration E-Cancellation
d. LOCAL	.00			Enter appropriate letter(s)
e. OTHER	.00	18. ESTIMATED DATE TO BE SUBMITTED TO FEDERAL AGENCY ▶ Year month day 19 X1 1 9	19. EXISTING FEDERAL IDENTIFICATION NUMBER	
f. TOTAL	$ 52,276 .00			

20. FEDERAL AGENCY TO RECEIVE REQUEST (Name, City, State, ZIP code)	21. REMARKS ADDED
U.S. Department of Education, Application Control Center, Washington, D.C. 20202	☐ Yes ☐ No

22. THE APPLICANT CERTIFIES THAT ▶
a. To the best of my knowledge and belief, data in this preapplication/application are true and correct, the document has been duly authorized by the governing body of the applicant and the applicant will comply with the attached assurances if the assistance is approved.
b. If required by OMB Circular A-95 this application was submitted, pursuant to instructions therein, to appropriate clearinghouses and all responses are attached: No response / Response attached
(1) ☐ ☐
(2) ☐ ☐
(3) ☐ ☐

23. CERTIFYING REPRESENTATIVE
a. TYPED NAME AND TITLE: Bartholomew Pressley, Pres
b. SIGNATURE: *Bartholomew Pressley*
c. DATE SIGNED Year month day 19 5 9

24. AGENCY NAME		25. APPLICATION RECEIVED Year month day 19
26. ORGANIZATIONAL UNIT	27. ADMINISTRATIVE OFFICE	28. FEDERAL APPLICATION IDENTIFICATION
29. ADDRESS		30. FEDERAL GRANT IDENTIFICATION

31. ACTION TAKEN	32. FUNDING		
☐ a. AWARDED	a. FEDERAL $ .00	33. ACTION DATE ▶ 19 Year month day	34. STARTING DATE 19 Year month day
☐ b. REJECTED	b. APPLICANT .00	35. CONTACT FOR ADDITIONAL INFORMATION (Name and telephone number)	
☐ c. RETURNED FOR AMENDMENT	c. STATE .00		36. ENDING DATE 19 Year month day
☐ d. DEFERRED	d. LOCAL .00		37. REMARKS ADDED
☐ e. WITHDRAWN	e. OTHER .00		
	f. TOTAL $ .00		☐ Yes ☐ No

38. FEDERAL AGENCY A-95 ACTION
a. In taking above action, any comments received from clearinghouses were considered. If agency response is due under provisions of Part I, OMB Circular A-95, it has been or is being made.
b. FEDERAL AGENCY A-95 OFFICIAL (Name and telephone no.)

ED Form 324-2, 9/84 (CFDA No. 84.016)   E6   STANDARD FORM 424 PAGE 1 (10-75) Prescribed by GSA, Federal Management Circular 74-7

Exhibit 19. Revised Budget Detail.

Anyville College Revised Budget	ED		TOTAL
A. Personnel			
1. Project Director in-kind overload (1 course)	0	2886	2886
2. 2 Faculty Group Leaders 1 term 1 course released time each	2806	4838	7644
3. 5 Faculty Participants in intro course (equivalent 1/4 course each)	7105		7106
4. 1 Faculty Released 1 course to teach Contemporary Latin American Literature in translation	2886		2886
5. 1 or 2 Faculty – 1 man month Summer work on computer-based language instruction	0	3800	3800
6. 7 Faculty including P.D. 5 for 1 week; 2 for 1-1/2 week at rate of 1/9 salary/month	7500		7500
7. Visiting Lecturer	3000		3000
Subtotal	23297	11524	34821
B. Fringe Benefits (18.4% S+W)	4287	2120	6407
C. Travel			
1. Consultant	975		975
2. Project Director	600		600
D. Equipment	0		0
E. Supplies			
1. Paper, binders, blank tapes, etc.	500		500
2. Library holdings	3200	500	3700
3. Duplicating	400		400
F. Contractual	0		
G. Construction	0		0
H. Other	0		0
1. Consultants	1000		1000
I. Total Direct Costs	34259	14144	48403
J. Indirect Costs (8% TDC)	2741	1132	3873
K. Project Total	37000	15276	52276

Exhibit 20. Federal Budget Form, Revised.

PART III — BUDGET INFORMATION

SECTION A — BUDGET SUMMARY

GRANT PROGRAM, FUNCTION OR ACTIVITY (a)	FEDERAL CATALOG NO. (b)	ESTIMATED UNOBLIGATED FUNDS		NEW OR REVISED BUDGET		
		FEDERAL (c)	NON-FEDERAL (d)	FEDERAL (e)	NON-FEDERAL (f)	TOTAL (g)
1. Undergrad International Studies and Foreign Language Program	84.016	$	$	$ 37,000	$ 15,276	$ 51,195

SECTION B — BUDGET CATEGORIES

6. OBJECT CLASS CATEGORIES	GRANT PROGRAM, FUNCTION OR ACTIVITY				TOTAL (5)
	(1) Federal	(2) Non-Federal			
a. PERSONNEL	$ 23,297	$ 11,524			$ 34,821
b. FRINGE BENEFITS	4,287	2,120			6,407
c. TRAVEL	1,575	--			1,575
d. EQUIPMENT	--	--			--
e. SUPPLIES	4,100	500			4,600
f. CONTRACTUAL	--	--			--
g. CONSTRUCTION					
h. OTHER	1,000	--			1,000
i. TOTAL DIRECT CHARGES	34,259	14,144			48,403
j. INDIRECT CHARGES	2,741	1,132			3,873
k. TOTALS	$ 37,000	$ 15,276			$ 52,276
7. PROGRAM INCOME					

Exhibit 21. Grant Award Notification.

U.S. DEPARTMENT OF EDUCATION
WASHINGTON, D.C. 20202

GRANTS AND CONTRACTS
SERVICE

GRANT AWARD NOTIFICATION

1	**RECIPIENT NAME** Anyville College 0000 South Street Anyville, E. Va. 00000	**4**	**AWARD INFORMATION** PR/AWARD NUMBER GOO---375 ACTION NUMBER 01 ACTION TYPE NEW AWARD TYPE DISCRETIONARY

2	**PROJECT TITLE** COST CONTAINMENT IN HIGHER EDUCATION: UNBUNDLING CHARGES TO STUDENTS DTD 03/07/88 AS AMENDED	**5**	**AWARD PERIODS** BUDGET PERIOD 09/01/X1 - 08/31/X2 PROJECT PERIOD 09/01/X1 - 08/31/X2

3	**PROJECT STAFF** RECIPIENT PROJECT DIRECTOR JANE DOE 20?- - EDUCATION PROGRAM STAFF EDNA GREEN 202- - EDUCATION GRANTS STAFF ANNE PERKING 202- -	**6**	**AUTHORIZED FUNDING** THIS ACTION $37,000 CARRY OVER -0- BUDGET PERIOD $37,000 PROJECT PERIOD $37,000 RECIPIENT COST SHARE $15,276
		7	**ADMINISTRATIVE INFORMATION** PAYMENT METHOD ED PMS ENTITY NUMBER 1-521244583-A1 REGULATIONS 34 CFR 74, 75, 77, 78 34 CFR 630 ATTACHMENTS AB

8	**LEGISLATIVE & FISCAL DATA** AUTHORITY: Higher EDUCATION AMENDMENTS OF 1980, P.L. 96-374, TITLE VI PROGRAM TITLE: FIPSE –UNDERGRADUATE INTERNATIONAL STUDIES CFDA: 84.016A

APPROPRIATION	FY	CAN	OBJECT CLASS	AMOUNT
9130201		E003088	4121	37,000

9	**TERMS AND CONDITIONS OF AWARD**
	
	THE FOLLOWING ITEMS ARE INCORPORATED IN THE GRANT AGREEMENT:
	   1) THE RECIPIENT'S APPLICATION (BLOCK 2),
	   2) THE APPLICABLE EDUCATION DEPARTMENT REGULATIONS (BLOCK 7).
	
	OTHER INFORMATION AFFECTING THIS ACTION IS PROVIDED IN THE ATTACHMENTS SHOWN IN BLOCK 7.

GRANTS OFFICER   B.R.BROWN   DATE

Ver. 1

ED - GCS 007 (9/87)   **PLEASE SEE OTHER SIDE FOR MORE INFORMATION**

Exhibit 22. Anyville Internal Grant Notification and Status Sheet.

TITLE OF PROJECT: Latin American Studies Program (Continuation)
AGENCY/ORGANIZATION
NAME: Department of Education
ADDRESS: 400 Maryland Avenue, SW, Washington, DC 20202
CONTACT/PROGRAM: Edna Green
CONTACT/FISCAL: Anne Perking - (202) 000-0000
PERIOD OF PROJECT: 09-01-00 TO 08-31-01
PERIOD OF AWARD: O9-01-00 TO 08-31-01
NEGOTIATED TERMS: Reduction
AMENDMENTS: Budget was revised on 05-09-00 for a request of $37,000.
AGENCY NO. G00000375   ANYVILLE ACCOUNT NO. #330. 000
PROJECT REPORT DUE: 11-30-00 PROJECT REPORT IN: 10-31-00
FISCAL REPORT DUE: 11-30-00 FISCAL REPORT IN: 11-31-00
AUTHORIZATIONS FOR PAYMENT
    1. PI/PD: Jane Doe
    2. Other:
    3. Sponsored Program Office: George Smith
    4. Fiscal Office: Susan S. Jones

NOTE: NO PAYMENTS CAN BE MADE WITHOUT ABOVE SIGNATURES.

Exhibit 23. Sample Vouchers.

REQUEST FOR PAYMENT EXTERNAL FUNDS	ANYVILLE COLLEGE SPONSORED PROGRAM	1. VOUCHER NO. 50		
2. CONSORTIUM: FISCAL AGENT	3. AGENCY/ORGANIZATION ED:Latin American Studies	4. AGENCY GRANT NO. G00 375		
5. SUBCONTRACTOR	6. PROJECT DIRECTOR (P.D.)/PRINCIPAL INVESTIGATOR (P.I.) Professor Doe	7. SBC ACCOUNT NO. 330.726		
8. PAYEE AND DESCRIPTION OR EXPLANATION *(ATTACH INVOICES OR PAYEE LIST)*		9. LINE ITEM	10. $ AMOUNT	
Pay to Mary I. Navarro for airfare for trip to ECC for consulting		C1	329	50

REQUEST FOR PAYMENT EXTERNAL FUNDS	ANYVILLE COLLEGE SPONSORED PROGRAM	1. VOUCHER NO. 57		
2. CONSORTIUM: FISCAL AGENT	3. AGENCY/ORGANIZATION ED:Latin American Studies	4. AGENCY GRANT NO. G00 375		
5. SUBCONTRACTOR	6. PROJECT DIRECTOR (P.D.)/PRINCIPAL INVESTIGATOR (P.I.) Professor Doe	7. SBC ACCOUNT NO. 330.726		
8. PAYEE AND DESCRIPTION OR EXPLANATION *(ATTACH INVOICES OR PAYEE LIST)*		9. LINE ITEM	10. $ AMOUNT	
Pay to John Hap for 2 weeks @ $650/week for teaching preparation		A1	1300	00

11. P.I./P.

14. SPON

REQUEST FOR PAYMENT EXTERNAL FUNDS	ANYVILLE COLLEGE SPONSORED PROGRAM	1. VOUCHER NO. 45		
2. CONSORTIUM: FISCAL AGENT	3. AGENCY/ORGANIZATION ED:Latin American Studies	4. AGENCY GRANT NO. G00 375		
5. SUBCONTRACTOR	6. PROJECT DIRECTOR (P.D.)/PRINCIPAL INVESTIGATOR (P.I.) Professor Doe	7. SBC ACCOUNT NO. 330.726		
8. PAYEE AND DESCRIPTION OR EXPLANATION *(ATTACH INVOICES OR PAYEE LIST)*		9. LINE ITEM	10. $ AMOUNT	
Pay to John Hap for teaching 4 classes for introductory Latin American Studies course (4 of 20 courses @ 1/7 salary per course) (4/20 * 1/7 * $45,981)		A1	1313	74
11. P.I./P.D. SIGNATURE *Jane Doe*	12. DATE 12/4	13. TOTAL CHARGED TO PROJECT	$ 1313	74
14. SPONSORED PROGRAM OFFICER'S SIGNATURE *George Smith*	15. DATE 12/6.	16. BUSINESS OFFICER'S SIGNATURE *Susan S Jones*		12/9/

11. P.I./P.I

14. SPON

Exhibit 24. Sample Spread Sheet.

ED: LATIN AMERICAN STUDIES   Grant #: G00 375
PD: Account #: 330726

Continuation: September 1, 19 - August 31, 19

Date	Payee	Voucher #	A1 Faculty Salaries	B Fringe Benefits	C1 Travel Consult.	C2 Travel PD	E1 Supplies	E2 Supplies Library	E3 Supplies Dup.	H Consultants	J Indirect Costs	TOTAL
			23297.00	4287.00	975.00	600.00	500.00	3200.00	400.00	1000.00	2741.00	37000.00
11/04/	Films/Humanities	38						69.75				69.75
11/06/	The Book Shop	39						314.38				314.38
11/06/	Library	40						1403.14				1403.14
12/04/	Seaman	41	702.17									702.17
12/04/	Edwards	42	782.89									782.89
12/04/	Moran	43	370.40									370.40
12/04/	Miller	44	1196.08									1196.08
12/04/	Hap	45	1313.74									1313.74
12/04/	Grimm	46	693.25									693.25
12/04/	Husz	47	187.55									187.55
01/10/	Duff	48	3000.00									3000.00
04/01/	Payroll	49	4000.00									4000.00
04/25/	Ing	50A				306.00						306.00
05/01/	Navarro	50			329.50							329.50
05/01/	Navarro	51								500.00		500.00
05/28/	Edwards	52	650.00									650.00
05/28/	Seaman	53	650.00									650.00
05/28/	Wit	54	650.00									650.00
05/28/	Lance	55	1300.00									1300.00
05/28/	Taylor	56	1300.00									1300.00
05/28/	Hap	57	1300.00									1300.00
05/28/	Rich	58	1300.00									1300.00
05/28/	Grimm	59	1300.00									1300.00
05/28/	Miller	60	1300.00									1300.00
05/28/	Ing	61	1300.00									1300.00
06/24/	Duplicating	62							77.11			77.11
06/24/		63		4286.48								4286.48
08/01/	Library Account	64						2348.60				2348.60
08/01/	Library Account	65						791.15				791.15
08/01/	Account 210375	66							536.81			536.81
08/21/		67									2741.00	2741.00
08/30/	BALANCE		.92	.52	645.50	294.00	500.00	-1727.02	-213.92	500.00	.00	.00

Exhibit 25. Financial Status Report to the Grantor.

FINANCIAL STATUS REPORT
(Short Form)
(Follow instructions on the back)

1. Federal Agency and Organizational Element to Which Report is Submitted	2. Federal Grant or Other Identifying Number Assigned By Federal Agency	OMB Approval No.	Page	of
U.S. Department of Education International Education Branch	Grant # G00---375	**0348–0039**	1	1 pages

3. Recipient Organization (Name and complete address; including ZIP code)
Anyville College
0000 South Street
Anyville, E.Va. 00000

4. Employer Identification Number	5. Recipient Account Number or Identifying Number	6. Final Report	7. Basis
000-000-0000-A1	Govt.Acct #330.726	☒ Yes ☐ No	☐ Cash ☒ Accrual

8. Funding/Grant Period (See Instructions) From: (Month, Day, Year)	To: (Month, Day, Year)	9. Period Covered by this Report From: (Month, Day, Year)	To: (Month, Day, Year)
09/01/ 19X1	08/31/19X2	09/01/19X1	08/31/19X2

10. Transactions:	I Previously Reported	II This Period	III Cumulative
a. Total outlays	–0–	–0–	$ 52,276
b. Recipient share of outlays	–0–	–0–	15,276
c. Federal share of outlays	–0–	–0–	37,000
d. Total unliquidated obligations			–0–
e. Recipient share of unliquidated obligations			–0–
f. Federal share of unliquidated obligations			–0–
g. Total Federal share (Sum of lines c and f)			37,000
h. Total Federal funds authorized for this funding period			37,000
i. Unobligated balance of Federal funds (Line h minus line g)			–0–

11. Indirect Expense

a. Type of Rate (Place "X" in appropriate box)
☐ Provisional ☒ Predetermined ☐ Final ☐ Fixed

b. Rate	c. Base	d. Total Amount	e. Federal Share
65%	S&W used 8%TDC	$3,873	$ 2,741

12. Remarks: Attach any explanations deemed necessary or information required by Federal sponsoring agency in compliance with governing legislation.

NOTE: Item 11.   This program limits indirect costs to 8% of total Direct Costs. Therefore, the predetermined rate of 65% S&W was not used.

13. Certification: **I certify to the best of my knowledge and belief that this report is correct and complete and that all outlays and unliquidated obligations are for the purposes set forth in the award documents.**

Typed or Printed Name and Title	Telephone (Area code, number and extension)
Ms Susan S. Jones, Vice President for Business Affairs (Chief Fiscal Officer)	20x-000-0000 ext 2

Signature of Authorized Certifying Official	Date Report Submitted
Susan S. Jones	09/31/19X2

Previous Editions not Usable

Standard Form 269A   (REV 4-88)
Prescribed by OMB Circulars A-102 and A-110

Evaluation

IMPORTANCE OF EVALUATION TO THE SPONSOR

Evaluation has become a *very* important requirement by most funding sources, private and government, for their own purposes. We have emphasized the importance of in-process evaluations as an essential tool for achieving the project objectives and preparing the basis for an after-the-fact or "summative" evaluation of the work. Now we will discuss the needs of the grantors. It is important for the grantors to know to what extent projects met expected goals. They will want information to help them determine what went right and what went wrong and why. Perhaps projects had unrealistic goals or perhaps external forces or unforeseen new information changed the expectations for the projects. Finally, the funding sources may want to learn if there was meaningful impact beyond the projects. If the projects resulted in publications or transferable plans, were these products cost effective and actually used by others with similar problems. The sponsors may be assessing the programs that provided the support. Should the programs be continued, revised, or abandoned in the light of the evaluations of all of their awards in a given field? Societal needs change and so do the priorities of government and private agencies charged with addressing urgent needs. One foundation officer told us "we have supported college level writing projects over the last three years. Now we need to evaluate our program based on the data provided from these grants and consider changing our priorities." In another case, a collection of data from well-managed successful projects may provide a persuasive argument for continuing to fund the current initiatives. We mention this to stress the importance of a carefully planned evaluation to a sponsor.

AN AGENCY REQUIREMENT FOR EVALUATION

The New Jersey Department of Higher Education explains in clear, concise terms what they expect of an evaluation plan. Many agencies are not explicit and simply list "evaluation" as one element of a proposal. The following evaluation requirements are from New Jersey's proposal solicitation guidelines:

Institutions are required to employ external, out-of-state evaluators for all funded projects as part of the evaluation process. The out-of-state evaluator must not be employed by or affiliated with any New Jersey higher education institution. The consultants are to assist the institutions in evaluating the projects with respect to achievement of the project's objectives, and to assist in the preparation of final reports. While these evaluation plans may vary in scope and design, they must contain provisions for the employment of external evaluators, and will be considered integral parts of the proposals. Consultants who assist with planning or implementing a funded project cannot be hired to evaluate the project.

The institution is not required to employ a different consultant for evaluating each project. If a number of projects are funded (through one or more Department of Higher Education Grant Programs), the institution may wish to coordinate the evaluation of the projects in order to permit a more comprehensive and effective review and to reduce the cost of consultant services.

To the extent possible, the complete results of the institution's evaluation should be submitted with the project's final report. If the evaluation process continues beyond the due date of the final report, the final report should specify the date on which the institution's evaluation will be submitted to the Department of Higher Education.

Evaluation plans should meet the following guidelines:

A. Procedures for data collection must be built into the project design so that data can be collected from the outset of the program.
B. Evaluation plans must consider both formative and summative assessments of the program. Data must be collected and analyzed to monitor progress in achieving project goals and to document the level of success in attaining these goals by the conclusion of the funding cycle.
C. Evaluation plans must include a balance of subjective indicators of participant satisfaction and objective indicators of project performance such as achievement test scores.
D. Evaluation plans should specify:

1. the data needed to assess the effectiveness of the actions taken to meet the project objectives;

2. the instruments and/or means to collect the data; and
3. the timetable for collection, analysis and report of the data.

PREPARING AN EFFECTIVE EVALUATION PLAN

One of the most difficult problems in planning and designing a project is that of providing for competent evaluation. Everyone wants the assurance that an evaluation is going to be carried out in some objective fashion, that the evaluation will justify continuation of the funding program, or justify continued support of similar kinds of activities or projects, or perhaps even call for ending an effort. We look at evaluation as a learning process both during the periods of planning and implementation and also on completion of a project. It is an important part of the theme of this book. A sincere and well-conceived, in-progress evaluation provides the information needed to alter plans, methods, and sometimes goals and thus helps to ensure a successful end result.

We are indebted to the late Dr. Sherry Lancaster who was a Research Associate with the State Council of Higher Education for Virginia when she planned the evaluation and served as the outside evaluator for the model evaluation we will use as an example later in this section. Start planning your evaluation by asking questions about the project objectives and plan of action.

1. What is the objective?
2. What information will have to be secured at the beginning before starting work, during the project, and after it is completed?
3. What are the sources of the needed information—participants, instructors, staff, other reports, databases, student records, etc.?
4. How will the information be collected—questionnaires, interviews, tests, other?
5. Who will be involved in the evaluation, planning, and implementation—an outside objective evaluator, the Project Director, participants, the sponsors—and what will be expected of each individual involved in the process?
6. When will each evaluation activity take place—choosing an outside evaluator, meetings with PI/PD and/or participant development of questionnaires, development of interview questions, distribution of questionnaires, scheduling of interviews?
7. What will be done with the data collected? Who will compile and analyze the information and how will it be done?

8. What will be done with the information—the raw data and analyses? Will they be required as separate reports, as part of brief summaries?

We found some universally good advice in the guidelines for the Fund for Improvement of Post Secondary Education (FIPSE) worth quoting here:

> What, in your view, would count as evidence that your project had succeeded? What would count as evidence that it had failed? It may be difficult, within the terms of the grant, to assess accomplishment of long-range objectives, but you should be able to identify or develop some proximate indicators. Bear in mind that the goals of local institutionalization and wide impact may well elude you unless you can provide others with solid evidence that your project achieved its aims. Developing such evidence should not be put off until the last stages of a project. It must be a consideration from the design stage onward . . . . Evaluation can be an important tool for increasing a project's wider use. In designing a good evaluation plan, it might help if you imagine that some other institution was submitting your proposal: what would you need to learn about their project in order for your institution to benefit concretely from its results? What form should the information take in order to be sufficiently noticeable, credible, and useful? Such evaluations typically use a combination of statistical measurement and non-quantitative evidence.

The FIPSE staff will provide a short bibliography of books and articles on evaluation. A written request should be sent to: U.S. Department of Education, Bibliography, Room 3100, 7th & D Streets, S.W., Washington, D.C. 20202-5175.

In summary, a competent evaluation during the progress of a project or after the fact should provide a measure of its success related to the original objectives, or expected outcomes, and even the unexpected outcomes. The failures and successes should be analyzed in terms of the methods, viewpoints of participants, and resulting products, e.g., publications, program formats.

AN EXAMPLE EVALUATION

We have chosen a community service project initiated and carried out by three colleges because it involves professors and administrators in those colleges and a wide range of community agencies in three counties and a small city.

Evaluation of "Central Virginia Tomorrow" (CVT)

The Central Virginia Tomorrow (CVT) project was one of the most ambitious projects for which Title I of the

Higher Education Act has provided support in Virginia. It met the Goals of Title I perfectly in that it began with the seed money Title I could provide and mushroomed into an extensive program involving leaders of industries, public agencies, colleges, and communities. It was decided to put great emphasis on "in-progress" evaluation of the project using a team comprised of two internal and two external evaluators. The Project Directors and Sponsored Program Officers of the colleges served as the internal contacts to insure use of the evaluation results to improve the program in progress. An objective outside evaluator developed the assessment plan. An outline of the actual evaluation procedure including the rationale for various actions, questionnaires, summaries, and analyses follows:

A meeting was held with the evaluation team to consider three major topics: (1) the project itself; (2) the evaluation process; and (3) resulting publication efforts.

The "internal" evaluators gave a briefing which included the following information:
1. Background of the problem
2. Participant groups in the project
   a. college-based people
   b. governmental agencies
   c. minority groups
   d. church groups
   e. business and industry
   f. civic organizations
3. Leaders of various community groups
4. Project format and design
5. Objectives of the project - 2 kinds
   a. Program objectives
      • to provide a forum for the leaders of the various local communities to share problems and ideas;
      • to enlist 50 to 100 people whose positions and relationships in their communities characterize them as leaders;
      • to provide these leaders with educational programs on environmental issues that will increase their awareness and understanding of environmental issues and lead them to voluntarily identify and work toward a solution to specific problems;
      • to provide students with the opportunity to employ skills and obtain experience in dealing with environmental problems with the measure of success being the development of accurate data for use in industry and local government;
      • to coordinate the training in community service agencies to provide a format for future agency training and to provide a sequence that will permit sequential development from basic skills through special advanced skills;
      • to develop a public awareness of the problems and activities that will have a visible result in terms of coordination of the regional community effort in problem identification and solution.
   b. Delivery system objectives
      • to establish a consortium council for continuing education and community service;
      • to establish a plan for pooling educational resources available among faculty, administrative personnel, and students to serve the plans of the council;
      • to establish an administrative procedure for the consortium to develop and administer projects for continuing education and community service;
      • to establish a permanent community advisory board for the consortium's continuing education and community service council.
6. Activities of the project
   a. Two Blacksburg conferences
   b. Five jurisdictional workshops
   c. Three seminars
   d. Numerous committee meetings for planning
7. Outcomes of the project so far
   a. Positive
   b. Negative
   c. Unexpected

After this internal evaluation briefing, work began on the evaluation process. There are two kinds of evaluation. One is an ongoing, formative evaluation during the progress of a program. The other is a final summation of the product. Both the process and the product evaluations should be integral parts of a project.

The formative evaluation provides information necessary to determine the extent to which a project is actually making gains toward achieving its objectives. It includes a documentation of what is occurring, reactions and perceptions of different participant groups, and a subsequent assessment as to how well the activities are helping to meet the goals and what changes might enhance this progress.

The product evaluation serves a different purpose. It is based on judgments regarding the general value of the total project after it has been completed, or after a segment of it has been completed. It provides information concerning the extent to which the goals have been attained; it also assesses unexpected side effects that may considerably enhance or, on the other hand, detract from the overall success of the project.

In this example it was decided that the greatest effort should be directed toward the "in-progress" evaluation and that the purpose of the evaluation should be to help the following types of people in various ways:

1. *administrators of funding sources*, to aid them in deciding which kinds of proposals and which projects to refund.
2. the *project director*, to aid him or her in making decisions concerning internal guidance and responding to requests from funding sources.
3. *program personnel*, to aid them by providing feedback required for effective carrying out of their duties.
4. *program participants*, to aid them in assessing the worthwhileness of their participation.
5. *policy makers*, to supply them with support for their efforts in setting or influencing policies.

It was also decided that the evaluation process should consist of both a questionnaire and personal interviews.

During the next few weeks the outside evaluator developed the questionnaire. Very few open ended questions were asked for two reasons: first, such questions take longer to answer, thereby decreasing the number of returns; second, answers to such questions are more difficult to analyze and interpret.

The questionnaire was reviewed by all members of the evaluation team. After one or two revisions the questionnaire was approved. (See Attachment A.)

The Project Director provided a list of names of the 206 people who had participated in at least one CVT program other than the jurisdictional workshops. Though only 100 questionnaires were needed to make up our 20% sample, the team decided to send them to all 206 to make sure that there would be enough returns, and self-addressed, stamped return envelopes were provided. Returns were requested by a deadline 10 days from date of mailing.

Within the ten-day period 116 returns were received, and over the next ten-day period 11 late responses came in. The tabulation of these appears as Attachment B.

A second meeting of the evaluation team was held with an agenda of three major items: 1) analysis and interpretation of the questionnaire replies we had received; 2) plans for interviews of participants; and 3) review of the first draft of our proceedings. A review of questionnaire responses showed trends and gaps in the information sought, which were important in planning for the interview phase.

It was decided the basic purpose of the interviews should be to obtain constructive criticism and suggestions for improvement. Therefore, we could use the questions on the questionnaire as a starting point, and then ask "why?" for more in-depth reactions. It was also decided that one person should conduct all the interviews in order to ensure uniformity. The team agreed that the outside evaluator should be that one person. Since all of the interviews would be conducted in some depth, it was agreed that a 5% random sample, or ten interviews would provide sufficient data.

The evaluator made appointments with the ten people in the random selection and scheduled 30 minutes for each interview. Permission was sought in advance to tape record the interviews. In order to ensure results suitable for comparative treatment, each person was asked the following questions:

1. What constructive criticisms do you have of CVT at this point?
2. What suggestions for improvement do you have for the project?
3. Why do you feel the majority of participants answering our questionnaire considered the first Blacksburg Conference the most valuable of all the meetings?
4. Why do you think the second Blacksburg Conference was attended less well?
5. Did you complete a questionnaire for us? If so, have you since changed you mind on any of your answers?

The interviews proved invaluable in getting to the reasons behind answers to the questionnaire. For example, one reason the second Blacksburg Conference had lower attendance turned out to be that hourly wage employees were having to take annual leave time without pay to attend any daytime meetings, and by spring they had used whatever time they felt they could afford and could not or did not take the two days off to go to Blacksburg a second time. Knowing this led several CVT leaders to consider a letter to certain employers asking if they would permit one of their employees to participate in the project without loss of leave or income. The leaders felt that in most cases if such employers received a letter of request accompanied by an explanation of CVT and signed by a key leader in the community, they would respond affirmatively.

The interviews brought out a number of repeated themes, specific suggestions, and specific complaints. These began to fit into patterns that could easily be summarized.

Exhibit 26. Sample Evaluation.

Attachment A
The Questionnaire

A team of evaluators is currently analyzing the Central Virginia Tomorrow Process in which you have participated. Your anonymous response to the following questions will help us to evaluate the project and see trends which emerge from the results. When we mention CVT below, we are referring to the process rather than the region. We would appreciate your response by April 14, 1975. Thank you.

1. In which of the following CVT programs have you participated: Please rank those you have attended in order of their significance to you. (1 - highest significance)
    ___ College A Seminar   ___ Blacksburg Conference
    ___ College B Seminar   ___ Jurisdictional Workshops
    ___ College C Seminar

2. If you have not attended all five of the above, what was your reason?
    ___ Dissatisfaction with a program   ___ Other (specify if you wish)
    ___ Conflict with a date

4. Which of the following groups do you feel are benefitting most from the CVT project?
    ___ The entire region   ___ Lower income people
    ___ Industrial leaders   ___ Middle income people
    ___ Community leaders   ___ Upper income people
    ___ College-based leaders   ___ County residents
    ___ Blacks   ___ City residents
    ___Whites

5. What do you feel has been the role of the Consortium Colleges in CVT?
    ___ Consistent significant leadership   ___ Consistent significant participation
    ___ Marginal involvement   ___ No real contribution

6. How much of the planning and accomplishment of CVT do you feel COULD have been attained without the project?
    ___ Nearly all of it   ___ A great deal of it
    ___ Very little of it   ___ Virtually none of it

7. How much of the planning and accomplishment of CVT do you feel WOULD have been attained without the project?

8. What do you feel was the basic purpose of CVT?
    ___ a. Getting representatives together from all segments of the region's population.
    ___ b. Identifying major issues and establishing specific roles.
    ___ c. Developing multi-media devices for region-wide education and revitalization.
    ___ d. Other—Specify.

9. How much of this purpose do you feel has been accomplished to date?
    ___ 0-25%   ___ 26-50%   ___ 51-75%   ___ 76-100%

10. What would you like to have seen CVT do differently?
    ___ Smaller meetings   ___ Larger meetings
    ___ More people involved   ___ Fewer meetings
    ___ More meetings   ___ Other (specify)

11. What would you like to see CVT become in the future?
    ___ A regional governmental organization   ___ A corporation   ___ Other (specify)
    ___ A volunteer steering committee

12. What unexpected occurrences have surfaced as a spin-off of CVT?

13. What specific impact has resulted from your participation in CVT?

14. Please classify yourself to help us identify patterns:
    ___ County resident   ___ Black   ___ Government employee
    ___ City resident   ___ White   ___ Private businessperson
    ___ Not gainfully employed

Exhibit 26. Sample Evaluation (cont.).

Attachment B
Responses to the Questionnaire

	1	2	3	4	5
1. A	21	13	16	7	3
B	4	10	10	9	11
RMWC	10	15	15	12	3
BLK	48	6	2	0	1
JW	14	20	8	9	3

2. Dissatisfied	5
Conflict	70
Other	23
3. Very much	52
Somewhat	46
Very little	12
4. Region	62
Industrial leaders	12
College based	15
Blacks	30
Whites	12
Lower income	23
Middle income	13
Upper income	12
County	12
City	29
Other	3–6 or more
5. Consistent leadership	49
Marginal	16
Consistent participation	54
None	3

6. All	11
Little	57
Great deal	26
None	17
7. All	5
Little	52
Great deal	13
None	38
8. a	49
b	70
c	7
d	9
9. 0-25	21
26-50	48
51-75	33
76-100	10
10. Smaller	21
More people	47
More meetings	14
Larger meetings	2
Fewer meetings	3
Other	25
11. Regional Govt.	15
Volunteer	56
Corporation	26
Other	13

Attachment C
Summary of Responses to Questionnaires

1. The majority of participants preferred the two-day Blacksburg conferences in the fall and spring to the one-day seminars or evening jurisdictional workshops.

2. Five participants indicated that they did not attend a CVT meeting because of dissatisfaction with the program. All others indicated that their lack of participation was due to conflict with the date or time.

3. Five participants felt only partially involved in the CVT process. Of these, two felt very little involved and three felt only somewhat involved. Four of these five were city-white participants.

4. The majority of participants felt that the region as a whole benefitted from the CVT process.

5. The role of the three colleges was perceived consistently as being positive.

6. 74 participants felt that very little or none of the CVT accomplishments could have been attained without the project.

7. 90 participants felt that very little or none of the CVT accomplishments would have been attained without the project.

8. Participants accurately perceived 8a. and 8b. as the basic purposes of CVT.

9. Participants felt that a range of 25-75% of CVT's objectives have been accomplished to date.

10. A majority of participants requested that more meetings be held.

11. 50% of the participants want to see a volunteer committee remain to steer CVT activities.

12. Specific answers by different groups of participants follow.

Exhibit 26. Sample Evaluation (cont.).

Responses to Question #12

What unexpected occurrences have you seen as a spin-off of CVT?

1. Business-City-White
   a. None (4 have this as their reply).
   b. Some people becoming involved who didn't expect to be part of such a planning group—also a spread of interest around the community.
   c. People do not want to deal with real problems.
   d. Regional information made known to City and County Representatives.
   e. Tremendous amount of information has been made available regarding areas of concern for both City and County.
   f. Some catalytic effect for minority business development.
   g. Black-White face-off.
   h. Strictly for the Blacks.
   i. Data for grant proposals.
   j. Possible development of new Black-operated business. New vision and hope on citizens' part.
   k. Industrial input and participation lost by having too much "talk" and not enough action.
   l. A better understanding between people.
   m. The ability to include all elements (people) from the region and have them work together.

2. Business-County-White
   a. None (3 gave this as their reply).
   b. Criticism of local government.
   c. Improved human relations and understanding of various problems.
   d. The Blacks won't move and are not ready to put much effort out.
   e. Realized need of inter-dependence in all areas and of all jurisdictions.
   f. Blue Sky thinking in too many areas. I did not realize how many people really don't understand some areas discussed—the people for the rural areas that must accept any plan for the most part were not present.

3. Business-County-Black
   a. A discovery of a common denominator whereby all segments of a given region can work together constructively to achieve a common goal.

4. Government-City-White
   a. I have seen more positive confrontation than I expected; County and City people at a roundtable, exchanging ideas; Minorities feeling that they have a part in determining priorities—better understanding of employer-employee problems—Human Relations.
   b. Group held together so far better than I expected.
   c. Curiosity to participation.

5. Government-City-Black
   a. Minority business enterprises organization.
   b. A common ground between participants who would never have talked about important issues without being involved in the process.

6. Government-County-White
   a. None (3 gave this as their reply)
   b. Greater citizens' participation in governmental operations than before CVT.
   c. A unity in purpose and goal-setting.
   d. The absence of the decision-makers.
   e. Good relationships between Black and White leadership.
   f. Many people involved for the first time in problem identification.
   g. "You-owe-us" attitude of Blacks; trend toward regional government; the selfish attitude of central city.

7. Other-City-White
   a. Not sure.
   b. A forum for the minorities.
   c. Several programs have been influenced by the CVT process.
   d. Greater awareness of what goes into solving problems that our governmental leaders are faced with.
   e. More cooperation—city/county.
   f. None.
   g. I could only see a strong force for regional government and the complete breakdown of elected form of government.

8. Other-County-White
   a. None.
   b. Agencies using concerns identified to develop current programs.
   c. Nothing particular.

9. Educator-City-White
   a. None.
   b. Participation and goal-sharing at local meetings among individuals who formerly would not or could not remain in the same room together. Individual recognition and acknowledgement of the views and rights of the other—by Black and White—industry and community.
   c. Bringing people together.
   d. Increased drug enforcement.

Exhibit 26. Sample Evaluation (cont.).

10. Educator-City-Black
   a. A surprising willingness for feuding political jurisdictions to talk to each other and AGREE on some basic things.
11. Educator-County-White
   a. People have gained a sense of the region and their interdependence on one another. Also, an awareness of some problems that have still to be dealt with (race relations and poverty, for example).
12. Educator-County-Black
   a. Not enough low-income persons participating (working class).
13. Student-City-White
   a. Nothing yet.

Responses to Question #13

What specific impact has resulted from your participation in CVT?
1. Business-City-White
   a. Nothing—none (4 persons gave these answers as their reply).
   b. Better informed, interested in areas which were pointed out as needing work.
   c. Chance to meet and work with other interested citizens.
   d. Acute awareness of problems and goals of City and County.
   e. Much more aware of City-County problems and goals and the cooperative effort that must be present to alleviate the problems.
   f. A new ray of hope that the region will work collectively to develop life-support systems which will work for all people and build a dynamic community with a high quality of life for all.
   g. Disheartened by changes—the public wants the government to pay—they are so uninformed.
   h. 80% of the population forgotten.
   i. Meet new people.
   j. Understanding of the issues before the people of the region, coming to know the region and some of its citizens, more awareness of the importance and need for formal planning for the future.
   k. Process is good but very frustrating because of the time it takes.
   l. Problem knowledge—lack of understanding by majority of citizens' realization.
   m. A heightened interest in regional cooperation; an expectation of success of regional improvement.

   n. Increased and renewed interest in regional development.
   o. Involvement in trust-awareness.
   p. Specific.
2. Business-County-White
   a. Awareness of high percent of public employees.
   b. Improved human relations and understanding of various problems.
   c. Health and business voice.
   d. Working together with diversified Central Virginia population segments.
   e. Know each problem better.
   f. More awareness of major issues. I am now more concerned about the region's future.
   g. The importance of an informed and concerned group of citizens, setting goals and working together in their attainment, has impressed me deeply.
   h. People have seen problems as having a regional basis.
   i. Realization that the different areas need to get together more in small groups and come to some realistic understanding on many issues, especially governments and government planning groups.
   j. I am more aware of the overlapping nature of the services and their interdependence and therefore of the complexity of the problem.
3. Business-County-Black
   a. An awareness of the ties between regional-city-county government and the importance of each working individually, yet collectively, to gain the best final result from any major change in a given area.
4. Government-City-White
   a. Upon me! Initial enthusiasm weakened by "group process" and evidence of provincialism leading to guarded pessimism. Upon others! Unknown.
   b. I have developed a greater understanding of the dilemma of the lower-income population of the area.
   c. Frustration because April is here and fear that once Blacksburg is over so will CVT be.
   d. More contacts with key people throughout region. It is to be hoped that more people will be made aware of the project including women in leadership and planning roles in the future.

Exhibit 26. Sample Evaluation (cont.).

e. Importance of involving people in determining problem, priorities, goals and such.

f. Our overall goals and objectives are much closer than I realized!

g. Met people I wouldn't otherwise have met from the area and beyond.

5. Government-City-Black

a. Realization of the region's potentials helped my individual outlook to be more realistic and not so negative.

6. Government-County-White

a. A better insight to the needs of the people.

b. More aware of problems in other jurisdictions.

c. A better understanding of the problems perceived by others in the community.

d. More respect for regional problems.

e. Became acquainted with more people from the region.

f. Only meeting a few new people and providing a forum for discussion.

g. A definite lack of interest on the part of those who really make things happen.

h. Confidence that we can work together for area problems.

i. Better understanding of the people, problems and possible solutions.

j. Once issues and goals are established, where does the funding come from?

k. Better understanding of the needs of the area.

7. Other-City-White

a. The conviction that such a project is possible.

b. A sense of involvement in what happens in the community (outside of my specific interest area), seeing the total CVT area not the city by itself.

c. Opportunity to learn about various aspects of the community and their relationships.

d. Involvement by my civic group.

e. Public looking with overview rather than none at all!

f. Immeasurable, due to the fact of my little involvement and chance for participation.

g. It has proved to me what I have always believed; that upper-class wants regional government.

8. Other-County-White

a. Greater awareness of community priority concerns.

b. Greater awareness of multiplying of problems—all interrelated—and the impact of small people in the community.

c. Made me aware that the entire area has similar problems, what benefits one county or city benefits the whole community.

d. Liberals want additional social problems.

9. Other-County-Black

a. I am sort of disappointed in the little evidence of change of opinion of members of the group from first meeting. The meetings seemed to have changed very few people in broadening their overview. The opinions expressed at the first group meetings were very much like the ones expressed at the final meeting. There seems to have been no broadening of the overview.

10. Educator-City-White

a. Growing conviction that a cross system approach can work.

b. I have a better insight into the problems facing all of us.

c. Closer working relationships and/or familiarity of nearly all participants.

d. Thinking there may be help for a region-wide approach to development of Central Virginia Tomorrow.

11. Educator-City-Black

a. Increased optimism that social problems can be solved.

12. Educator-County-Black

a. I have gained greater insight on long-range planning, as well as a better understanding of how some problem areas are left out of plans.

b. Problem areas are left out of plans.

13. Student-City-White

a. An acute awareness of the problems of the Central Virginia region.

b. Learning about the region; getting to know people; getting involved.

14. Student-City-Black

a. Virginia has some of the same problems that other states have. That is, although we are in the south, we still have some of the problems found in the west. Problems are not confined to geographical location.

Exhibit 26. Sample Evaluation (cont.).

Attachment D

QUESTION #4 RECAP:

PERCEPTIONS OF WHO IS BENEFITTING MOST FROM CVT

	GOVERNMENT EMPLOYEES			
	City		*County*	
	Black	*White*	*Black*	*White*
1. The entire region	1	5	2	8
2. Industrial leaders	0	1	1	0
3. Community leaders	2	6	1	7
4. College-based leaders	0	2	0	2
5. Blacks	0	4	2	3
6. Whites	1	2	1	0
7. Lower income people	0	4	1	3
8. Middle income people	1	2	0	0
9. Upper income people	0	2	0	2
10. County residents	0	1	0	1
11. City residents	0	3	1	3
12. Other	0	1	0	

	PRIVATE BUSINESSPEOPLE			
	City		*County*	
	Black	*White*	*Black*	*White*
1. The entire region	0	19	1	5
2. Industrial leaders	0	3	0	2
3. Community leaders	0	8	0	7
4. College-based leaders	0	6	0	1
5. Blacks	0	4	0	6
6. Whites	0	2	0	0
7. Lower income people	0	4	0	5
8. Middle income people	0	1	0	2
9. Upper income people	0	3	0	1
10. County residents	0	2	0	1
11. City residents	0	6	0	7
12. Other	0	0	0	3

Exhibit 26. Sample Evaluation (cont.).

| | EDUCATORS | | | |
| | City | | County | |
	Black	White	Black	White
1. The entire region	2	5	0	1
2. Industrial leaders	1	1	0	0
3. Community leaders	1	1	0	1
4. College-based leaders	1	0	0	0
5. Blacks	1	1	0	0
6. Whites	1	0	0	1
7. Lower income people	1	1	0	0
8. Middle income people	1	1	0	0
9. Upper income people	1	1	1	1
10. County residents	1	1	0	0
11. City residents	1	1	0	1
12. Other	0	0	0	0

| | OTHERS | | | |
| | City | | County | |
	Black	White	Black	White
1. The entire region	1	7	0	1
2. Industrial leaders	1	1	0	1
3. Community leaders	1	7	1	1
4. College-based leaders	1	2	0	1
5. Blacks	1	4	0	1
6. Whites	2	1	0	0
7. Lower income people	1	1	0	1
8. Middle income people	1	3	0	0
9. Upper income people	0	1	0	0
10. County residents	2	4	0	1
11. City residents	2	4	0	1
12. Other				

Figure 23. Sample Evaluation (cont.).

Attachment E
QUESTION #11 RECAP:
WHAT DIFFERENT GROUPS WOULD LIKE TO SEE CVT BECOME

GOVERNMENT EMPLOYEES

	City		County	
	Black	White	Black	White
A regional governmental organization	3	2	0	2
A volunteer steering committee	0	50	9	
A corporation	0	5	2	2
Other	0	1	0	3

PRIVATE BUSINESSMEN

	City		County	
	Black	White	Black	White
A regional governmental organization	0	5	0	2
A volunteer steering committee	0	15	0	10
A corporation	0	7	1	3
Other	0	2	0	4

EDUCATORS

	City		County	
	Black	White	Black	White
A regional governmental organization	0	2	1	2
A volunteer steering committee	0	1	0	0
A corporation	1	2	0	0
Other	0	0	0	1

OTHERS

	City		County	
	Black	White	Black	White
A regional governmental organization	0	1	0	1
A volunteer steering committee	0	8	1	3
A corporation	0	5	0	3
Other	0	1	0	0

Attachment F
SUMMARY OF INTERVIEWS
Repeated Themes

1. City people are very aware that county people are saying "CVT is a Lynchburg show."
2. Continued meetings are important to keep CVT participants informed and interested in implementation.
3. Lynchburg's "track record" includes numerous planning meetings but few outcomes; the hope is that CVT will implement as well as it has planned.
4. More media coverage is needed to inform more people of CVT's purposes, goals, and activities.
5. Periodic reports should go to all participants to keep them updated on progress and make them feel important to the process.
6. Bedford County is the most vocal critical participant; Appomattox is the most apathetic.

Exhibit 26. Sample Evaluation (cont.).

7. The Blacksburg Conferences were of great value in getting people's total time commitment to CVT for a longer period of time.

8. One of the greatest accomplishments of CVT has been to get people together to communicate their community and regional concerns to each other.

9. There is great hope that CVT will "keep moving," because it is beneficial to so many specific interests to continue to communicate and work for the future.

10. CVT is at a crucial point now, and great care must be taken to ensure its continuation.

11. CVT must attempt in any way possible to keep the top people involved in CVT, because their participation signifies top-level interest which others will follow.

12. Lynchburg College has been the most active in working with the community; RMWC has been the least.

13. CVT has provided a vehicle for relieving many suspicions held by the community towards academics.

Specific Suggestions

1. A detailed study phase should precede the implementation of any CVT recommendations, because participants do not always know the consequences of their suggestions.

2. Committee chairs and committees of each interest area (i.e., housing, education, etc.) should have an update meeting to inform participants of where they are now and where they're going. This could be in the form of a Dutch treat lunch.

3. A report should be sent to all CVT participants to inform them of the plans made by the organizational committee at the Peaks of Otter.

4. More people under 30 and not yet established should be included—as observers if not as full participants.

5. The interest and participation of each organizational committee member should be checked; if anyone hasn't the time to devote to meeting and planning, he should be replaced by someone who can be a full participant.

6. Make clear whether the CVT meetings are open to the public or by invitation only.

7. Hold more meetings in the evenings to involve more "grass roots" people. These people are not able to leave their jobs for full days to attend CVT meetings.

8. Alleviation of the drug problem should be a goal in itself rather than being considered a part of law enforcement.

9. More of the "right" people must be involved; specifically, more agency directors, more civic group leaders, and judges.

10. After sub-groups meet to discuss different issues in workshops, enough time should be left for all participants to get back together as a whole and be able to reach to the sub-groups' reports.

11. CVT could have a form letter that would go out to employers of the "little" people, requesting the employers to support CVT by giving these "little" people time off with pay and without losing annual leave to attend CVT meetings.

12. CVT should send out notices of meetings sooner than they have in the past.

13. One way to increase awareness and publicity of CVT is to set up a speakers' bureau to visit all regional civic groups periodically.

14. Give the counties more representation in CVT, and accomplish this by election rather than selection to the board of directors.

Specific Complaints

1. CVT is really a Lynchburg project—not a regional one.

2. Bedford has not given CVT a chance; it cannot see ahead.

3. The colleges are taking on too much leadership and community people are suspicious that they are being "manipulated."

4. The economist who spoke at college B's seminar was irrelevant, unprepared, and turned people off CVT.

5. Too many meetings were held on workdays. Only executives and owners of businesses had the kinds of jobs they could leave for this long. This is the reason attendance was down at the second Blacksburg Conference.

6. Enough top-level influential leaders are still not being convinced to lend their full support to the CVT process.

7. Reports of group meetings have not always been accurate summaries of what has actually occurred.

8. Outside speakers have not always been as effective or as relevant as local experts could be.

9. Title I, and the three colleges, have not received enough credit for their roles in CVT.

10. The counties are very fearful of the use of federal money for any reason, because federal dollars are bound to be accompanied by federal intervention.

The evaluation of the CVT project demonstrated the importance of involving all of the constituents in the process of planning and reviewing progress toward the original goals. The in-process or formative evaluation technique helped reveal shortcomings and new ideas while there was still time to change course. The commu- nity planning process was successfully started and the information compiled would provide a solid basis for future community development. The evaluation process itself was an important contributor to the project's suc- cess.

Conclusion

We have attempted to lead you through a complete process for nurturing an idea from its inception to its conclusion, the conclusion being the result of an evaluation of the project's impact. Common sense dictated much of what we have written about developing a competitive proposal. Spending the sponsors', and sometimes the taxpayers' dollars, and taking an honest look at the impact of your project are responsibilities to be taken very seriously.

The sections that follow include reference materials mentioned in the text and other useful, if not essential, information. No one guide to proposal development can provide all of the answers. We have attempted to provide you with a selection of actual forms and regulations that you can use to track down current versions or those that fit your mission.

We have fortified the text with actual examples and case studies that are adaptable to other real situations. These examples are only one way of doing the job. The management system described could be adopted for a small organization with little change. If you are not handy with computer spread sheets, hand posted accounts are still acceptable. The evaluation we selected gives a thorough picture of a project and its accomplishments and flaws. One feature that led us to choose this example was the outside evaluator's effective use of the insiders in the evaluation. This was a team effort from the beginning and using insiders was very important to the in-process assessment so essential to the success of any new venture.

Thorough and thoughtful planning, involving others in your plans and articulating the plans to bring your "idea" to fruition in clear, concise, jargon-free English will lead you to success.

Don't give up. Good ideas will eventually be recognized and implemented if they are clearly articulated and have genuine support from those they affect.

Let us conclude with the school motto of one of the authors.

"Inveniam viam aut faciam"

translated

"I will find a way or make one"

PART II: BASIC RESOURCES

Section I. Acronyms

AAAS American Association for the Advancement of Science

AAHA American Association for the Humanities Administration

AAC Association for American Colleges

ACE American Council on Education

ACLS American Council for Learned Societies

ACS American Chemical Society

ACUO Association of College and University Offices, Inc.

ADAMHA Administration on Drug Abuse, Mental Health and Alcoholism

AFOSR Air Force Office of Scientific Research

AOA Administration on Aging

ARI Army Research Institute

ARO Army Research Office

BARC Beltsville Agricultural Research Center

CASE Council for the Advancement and Support of Education

CBD Commerce Business Daily

CFDA Catalog of Federal Domestic Assistance

CFR Code of Federal Regulations

CIES Council for the International Exchange of Scholars

CPB Corporation for Public Broadcasting

CURI College-University Resource Institute, Inc.

DEA Drug Enforcement Administration

DOT Department of Transportation

ED Education Department or Department of Education

EDGAR Education Department General Administrative Regulations

EEOC Equal Employment Opportunity Commission

EPA Environmental Protection Agency

ERIC Education Resources Information Clearinghouse

ESEA Elementary and Secondary Education Act

FIPSE Fund for the Improvement of Post Secondary Education

FOB# Federal Office Building number

FONZ Friends of the National Zoo

GAO Government Accounting Office

GPO Government Printing Office

GSA General Services Administration

HEA Higher Education (Act) Amendments

HED Higher Education Daily

HENA Higher Education and National Affairs

HHS Health and Human Services (Department of)

HUD Housing and Urban Development (Department of)

ICA International Communications Agency

IMF International Monetary Fund

IPA Intergovernmental Personnel Act

IREX International Research and Exchange Board

LSCA Library Services and Construction Act

MDTA Manpower Development and Training Act

NACUBO National Association of College and University Business Officers

NASA National Aeronautics and Space Administration

NBS National Bureau of Standards

NCES National Center for Educational Statistics

NCURA National Council of University Research Administrators

NDEA National Defense Education Act

NEA National Endowment for the Arts and/or National Education Association

NEH National Endowment for the Humanities

NHPRC National Historical Publications and Records Commission

NIA National Institute on Aging

NIAAA National Institute on Alcohol Abuse and Alcoholism

NIDA National Institute on Drug Abuse

NIH	National Institutes of Health	**ONR**	Office of Naval Research
NIHR	National Institute for Handicapped Research	**OSHA**	Occupational Safety and Health Administration
NIJ	National Institute of Justice	**OTA**	Office of Technology Assessment
NIMH	National Institute of Mental Health	**PHS**	Public Health Service
NLRB	National Labor Relations Board	**SRA**	Society of Research Administrators
NOAA	National Oceanic and Atmospheric Administration	**SSRC**	Social Science Research Council
NRC	Nuclear Regulatory Commission		
NSF	National Science Foundation		
NSFRE	National Society of Fund Raising Executives		
NTIA	National Telecommunication and Information Administration		
OCD	Office of Child Development		
OCR	Office of Civil Rights		
OMB	Office of Management and Budget		

Other abbreviations of interest:

ASAP	As Soon As Possible
FY	Fiscal Year
FYI	For Your Information
NA	Not Applicable
PTO	Please Turn Over
RFP	Request for Proposal
RFA	Request for Applications

Section II. Essential Basic Information Sources

A. PUBLICATIONS

In establishing a basic resource library for your organization, a number of points should be considered. First and foremost is that the library represents the needs of your agency in four areas:

1. Basic library or reference sources.
2. Periodicals from agencies and foundations.
3. Periodicals from private/professional sources.
4. Information services that provide a basic information packet, along with possible periodic update services.

Additionally, cost should be a factor in what your library will include. For instance, a low-budget office might consider having the following holding for under $250.

	Price or range
Foundation Directory	$140.
Catalog of Federal Domestic Assistance	38.
News, Notes and Deadlines	60.
NIH Guide for Grants and Contracts	FREE
NSF Bulletin	FREE
Humanities	20.
Federal Agency Directories/Reports	FREE
Foundation Newsletters and Annual Reports (i.e., Ford, Carnegie, Rockefeller)	FREE

In addition you might consider subscribing to the *Federal Register* at $340 per year if federal programs are your primary interest. And you might consider purchasing the annual *Directory of Research Grants* ($118).

Write to those agencies that deal with your particular interests and ask for their newsletters, reports, and related lists of programs and guidelines. There is nothing wrong with seeking general information in more detail than that offered by the *Foundation Directory* and the *Catalog of Federal Domestic Assistance*, but do not send proposals off at this point. We are merely pointing out how to gather information if your resources and technical support are limited.

B. NEWS RELEASES

Here is a list of federal agencies with programs of interest to educational institutions that send out news releases to those on their mailing list. In addition to the correct name, the only address you need is Washington, DC, plus the zip code.

> Department of Agriculture (USDA) 20505
> Department of Education (ED) 20202
> Department of Energy (DOE) 20585
> Department of Health and Human Services (HHS) 20201
> Department of Labor (DOL) 20210
> Department of Transportation (DOT) 20594
> Environmental Protection Agency (EPA) 20460
> National Endowment for the Arts (NEA) 20506
> National Endowment for the Humanities (NEH) 20506
> National Institutes of Health (NIH) 20014
> National Science Foundation (NSF) 20550
> Smithsonian Institution (SI) 20560

C. TELEPHONE BOOKS

An often overlooked source of information is the Washington, DC, (or any city) telephone book. The most frequently called agency numbers appear in "The Blue Pages," which list state, District of Columbia, and federal government numbers and local addresses. Under each agency a number of special phone numbers are listed as well as a general information number that can help direct your call to the appropriate section or office. At the beginning of "The Blue Pages" section is a list of about 25 of the most frequently called numbers.

Telephone numbers within a federal agency are listed in its own directory and are largely for internal use. The directory of the National Science Foundation is made available to those with a need and the National Endowment for the Humanities lists key numbers in its program guide. Most agency directories can be purchased through the Government Printing Office. At one time or another most agencies have a phone book in print and available through the Government Printing Office by mail or one of its book stores.

D. GOVERNMENT PRINTING OFFICE (GPO) LIST OF PUBLICATIONS

Familiarity with GPO and its publications is essential. Visit the GPO Bookstore, if you come to Washington, or one of the branch stores. It is worth checking to see if there is a branch nearby. If you want current information on government publications, GPO sends out a list monthly. It is titled "Selected U.S. Government Publications." Check your local library to see how to order from GPO or simply write for an order form and the monthly listing.

Section III. Other Sources of Assistance and Training

Your institution or organization may belong to some national organizations that provide guidance and information on federal programs. Below is a list of such national organizations that, though incomplete, will give you an idea of what might be available to your institution and to you.

If you are associated with a community college, a land-grant college, or a large health organization, chances are you will find a staff member who has information on government funding and other sources with interests directly related to the association's membership. There are experienced people in these national offices, and the government agency program officers know and respect them. In other cases, state systems provide assistance to faculty and individual campuses.

A. PARTIAL LIST OF EDUCATION ORGANIZATIONS

These organizations can be reached at (1) and (11) Dupont Circle NW, Washington, DC 20036 (area code 202). (A complete list with names of key personnel is available from CASE for $6.00. See Section V, Annotated Bibliography, under Higher Education Directory).

American Association for Higher Education (AAHE)	(1) 293-6440
American Association of Colleges for Teacher Education (AACTE)	(1) 293-2450
American Association of Colleges of Nursing (AACN)	(11) 463-6930
American Association of Community and Junior Colleges (AACJC)	(1) 728-0200
American Association of State Colleges and Universities (AASCU)	(1) 293-7070
American Council on Education (ACE)	(1) 939-9300
American Society for Engineering Education (ASEE)	(11) 293-7080
American Society of Allied Health Professions (ASAHP)	(1) 293-3422
Association of American Medical Colleges (AAMC)	(1) 828-0400
Association of American Universities (AAU)	(1) 466-5030
Association of Catholic Colleges and Universities	(1) 457-0650
Association of Governing Boards of Universities and Colleges (AGB)	(1) 296-8400
Association of University Programs in Health Administration (AUPHA)	(1) 659-4354
Council for Advancement and Support of Education (CASE)	(11) 328-5900
Council of Graduate Schools in the U.S. (CGS)	(1) 223-3791
Council of Independent Colleges (CIC)	(1) 466-7230
Educational Resources Information Center Clearinghouse on Higher Education (ERIC/HE)	(1) 296-2597
Educational Resources Information Center Clearinghouse on Teacher Education (ERIC/TE)	(1) 293-2450
Higher Education Policy and Administration Library and Information Service (HEPALIS)	(1) 833-4690
Law School Admission Council (LSAC)	(11) 387-5750
National Association of College and University Attorneys (NACUA)	(1) 296-0207

National Association of College and University Business Officers
(NACUBO)   (1) 861-2500
National Association of State Universities and Land-Grant Colleges
(NASULGC)   (1) 778-0818
National Council of University Research Administrators (NCURA)   (1) 466-3894
National University Continuing Education Association (NUCEA)   (1) 659-3130

B. OTHER WASHINGTON METROPOLITAN AREA ADDRESSES:

(Washington, DC, unless otherwise indicated)

American Assembly of Collegiate School of Business (AACSB), Suite 320,
1755 Massachusetts Avenue, NW, 20036   483-0400
American Association for Advancement of Science (AAAS), 1333 H Street,
NW, 20005   326-6400
American Association of University Professors (AAUP), Suite 500, 1012 14th
Street, NW, 20005   737-5900
American Association of University Women (AAUW), 2401 Virginia Avenue,
NW, 20037   785-7700
American Chemical Society (ACS), Suite 701, 1155 16th Street, NW,
20036   872-4600
Association of Academic Health Centers (AHC), Suite 410, 1400 16th Street,
NW, 20036   265-9600
Association of American Colleges (AAC), 1818 R Street, NW, 20009   387-3760
Association of American Law Schools (AALS), Suite 800, 1201 Connecticut
Avenue, NW, 20036   296-8851
Association of College and University Offices, Inc. (ACUO), Suite 901,
1001 Connecticut Avenue, NW, 20036   659-2104
Association of Jesuit Colleges and Universities (AJCU), 1717 Massachusetts
Avenue, NW, 20036   667-3888
Association of Physical Plant Administrators of Universities and Colleges
(APPA), 1446 Duke Street, Alexandria, VA 22314-3492   703-684-1446
College and University Personnel Association (CUPA), Suite 503, 1233 20th
Street, NW, 20036   429-0311
Council for International Exchange of Scholars (CIES), Suite M500, 3400
International Drive, NW, 20008-3097   686-4000
Council on Library Resources, Inc. (CLR), Room 313, 1785 Massachusetts
Avenue, NW, 20036   483-7474
Foundation Center, 1001 Connecticut Avenue, NW (3rd Floor),
20036   331-1400
International Council on Education for Teaching (ICET), Suite 609, 2009
North 14th Street, Arlington, VA 22201   703-543-9111
Lutheran Resources Commission (LRC-W), 5 Thomas Circle, NW, 20005   667-9844
National Association for Equal Opportunity in Higher Education
(NAFEO), 2243 Wisconsin Avenue, NW, 20007   333-3855
National Association of Independent Colleges and Universities (NAICU),
Suite 750, 122 C Street, NW, 20001   347-7512
National Association of Student Financial Aid Administrators (NASFAA),
Suite 100, 1776 Massachusetts Avenue, NW, 20036   785-0453
National Education Association (NEA),1201 16th Street, NW, 20036   833-4000
National Home Study Council, 1601 18th Street, NW, 20009   234-5100

Section IV. Forms and Required Information

It would probably be most helpful—or at least less confusing—if every federal agency used the same application forms. Unfortunately, this is not the case, not because of any predetermined obstinacy on the part of federal agencies, but primarily because each application form was developed to provide the unique information an agency believes it needs to process proposals.

However, there is some information that seems to repeat itself from application form to application form, and there is certain unique information that certain agencies require each time an application is submitted. In this section we have provided examples of current application forms for federal agencies that educational, training, and research institutions are most likely to be applying to for project support. In addition, we have listed some of the standard and special institutional information needed to complete each form.

While the information provided should be most helpful in completing the forms, this appendix should not be viewed as all-inclusive. It is only a reference tool to be used when preparing an application. The best sources of specific information are the sponsoring agencies' application kits. Still, we hope this additional information will help with the sometimes confusing task of "filling out the forms."

One thing to keep in mind, many government forms are copied from copies and the small print is often illegible (as with some of the examples in this section). When first quality printed forms run low, usually when a revised version is pending, you may find you have to copy the copy of the copy. If you are concerned about the small print, call the agency and ask for a readable copy. The last time we did this, the unreadable was read to us: "Do not write in this space—Internal use only."

A. CLASSIFICATION OF TYPES OF GRANT APPLICATIONS

Exhibit 27. Types of Grant Applications.

CLASSIFICATIONS OF TYPES OF GRANT APPLICATIONS				
TYPES	DEFINITIONS	DISTINGUISHING FEATURE	LIMITATIONS	NON-GOV'T* REVIEW REQUIRED
NEW	An action which is being submitted by an applicant for the first time	Not previously submitted	Availability of funds, Successful competition based upon published evaluation criteria	Yes
CONTINUATIONS	A grant application which contains multiyear documentation and the original grant contemplated multiyear funding	Multiyear scope and budget	Funds are available, Successful prior year performance, Continuation is in the best interest of the Government	No
COMPETING CONTINUATIONS	A grant application which proposes to continue an existing grant beyond the grant period on year-to-year basis	Year-to-year application is required; treated the same as a new application	Availability of funds, Successful competition based upon published evaluation criteria	Yes
COMPETING EXTENSION GRANT	The first grant made in support of the project period extension, requested on a competing extension application	Multiyear project period following a multiyear project period	Availability of funds, Successful completion of prior project period	Yes
SUPPLEMENTAL GRANT	An action which pertains to an increase in the amount of the Federal contribution for the for the same period	Funding increase, No time extension	Availability of funds Program judgment priorities	No
CHANGES IN THE EXISTING GRANT	Increase in duration Decrease in duration Decrease in Federal Funding	Grant period changes Federal contribution decreases only	No funding increases	No

* For the purpose of this directive "Non-Government" means Non-Federal

B. DEPARTMENT OF DEFENSE (DOD)

General

Although DOD may give grants, it usually funds unsolicited research proposals via the mechanism of a contract. The Short Form Research Contract, DD Form 2222-2, has a format that allows the applicant to make an "offer" and for the government to accept it. The form is easy to complete. The only area that may cause confusion is that, because it is an offer, they ask for the name of the technical and administrative representatives authorized by the institution to conduct negotiations.

Exhibit 28. DOD Short Form Research Contract.

SHORT FORM RESEARCH CONTRACT RESEARCH PROPOSAL COVER PAGE		
DATE SUBMITTED		**DO NOT USE THIS BLOCK**

1. TO *(Submit ___ copies of proposal to)*	2. FROM *(Name and address of offeror)*
a. NAME	a. NAME
b. ADDRESS *(Street, City, State, Zip)*	b. ADDRESS *(Street, City, State, Zip)*
	c. IDENTIFICATION NUMBER

3. SCIENTIFIC FIELD	4. TYPE OF ORGANIZATION *(X one)*
	a. Educational Institution
	b. Other nonprofit

5. TITLE OF PROPOSAL	6. PROPOSAL ALSO BEING SUBMITTED TO

7. PROPOSED AMOUNT $	8. REQUESTED DURATION

9. REQUESTED START DATE *(YYMMDD)*	10. TYPE OF CONTRACT *(X one)*
	a. Cost Plus Fixed Fee
11. PROPOSAL VALID UNTIL *(Minimum 6 months)*	b. Cost, No Fee
	c. Cost Sharing

12. PRINCIPAL INVESTIGATOR(S)

a. Name	b. Department	c. Telephone Number
(1)		
(2)		
(3)		

13. ADMINISTRATIVE REPRESENTATIVE AUTHORIZED TO CONDUCT NEGOTIATIONS

a. Name	b. Department	c. Telephone Number
(1)		
(2)		

14. OFFEROR'S STATEMENTS *(See Page 2)* *(Write enclosures or page numbers in appropriate block. If page numbers, precede item(s) by "pg")*

a. Technical

(1) Title and abstract of proposed effort	
(2) Statement of Work	
(3) Discussion of background, objectives, approaches, and available facilities	
(4) Names and brief biographical information of key personnel	

b. Financial

(1) Cost estimate detailed by cost elements on SF 1411 or equivalent	
(2) Type of support other than financial, if any, required of the Government, e.g., facilities, equipment, materials, or personnel resources	

c. Administrative

(1) Statements, if applicable, regarding cost sharing, organizational conflicts of interest, status of security clearances, environmental impact, and previous or organizational experience in the field covered by the proposal.	
(2) Statement as to why it is necessary to acquire property, if any, with contract funds (See FAR 45.302)	

15. AUTHORIZED REPRESENTATIVE

a. Typed Name	b. Signature
c. Title	d. Date Signed *(YYMMDD)*

DD Form 2222-2, 84 APR   Previous editions are obsolete

Exhibit 28. DOD Short Form Research Contract (cont.).

SHORT FORM RESEARCH CONTRACT RESEARCH PROPOSAL
PAGE 2

14. OFFEROR'S STATEMENTS

a. USE AND DISCLOSURE OF DATE *(X one)*

(1) Except as indicated in (2) below, the proposal shall not be duplicated, used, or disclosed outside the Government in whole or in part for any purpose other than to evaluate the proposal without the written permission of the offeror (Except that if a contract is awarded on the basis of this proposal, the terms of this contract shall control disclosure and use). This restriction does not limit the Government's right to use information contained in the proposal if it is obtainable from another source without restriction. All data contained in this proposal is subject to this restriction unless specifically excluded by the offeror. Permission is hereby granted to evaluate this proposal in accordance with your normal procedures which may include evaluation by evaluators both within and outside the Government with the understanding that written agreement not to disclose this information shall not be required of or obtained from any such evaluators.

(2) Restrict the evaluation of the above proposal to Government personnel only. The offeror shall mark the proposal in accordance with FAR 15.509.

b. CONTRACT CLAUSES

By signature on Page 1 of this Proposal, the offeror authorizes award of a contract in accordance with the provisions of DFARS 35.70 and agrees to be bound by the contract clauses contained in DFARS 52.235-7005, in effect on the date of this proposal, or such other date as may be mutually agreed upon.

c. REPRESENTATIONS AND CERTIFICATIONS *(X one)*

(1) Representations and Certifications pertaining to Contingent Fee Representation and Agreement, Certification of Nonsegregated Facilities, Previous Contract Compliance Reports, Affirmative Action Compliance, and Clear Air and Water Certification, Organizational Conflicts of Interest, and Insurance Immunity From Tort Liability were furnished your office on *(Enter date)* _____
These representations and certifications remain valid and are appropriate for the subject proposal. No facility to be used for the proposed research has been the subject of a conviction under the Clean Air Act or the Federal Water Pollution Act.

(2) The comprehensive Representations and Certifications as cited above have not been submitted. The attached Representations and Certifications have been developed in connection with the subject proposal and *(X one)*

(a) should be used only in connection with the subject proposal.

(b) may be used not only for the subject proposal but as a comprehensive submission for possible use with prospective unsolicited proposals.

d. ADVANCE PAYMENTS *(Applicable only to offerors with existing payment agreements with DOD)*

Advance payments will be made for performance of this SFRC pursuant to the terms and conditions of the Advance Payment Pool Agreement dated *(Enter date)* _____ between the Department of *(Enter name)* _____ and the contractor. *(Enter name)* _____
The provisions of that Agreement are hereby incorporated by reference in this SFRC with the same force and effect as though fully set forth herein. If this SFRC is awarded by the Department that entered into the Advance Payment Pool Agreement with the Contractor, this SFRC shall be paid by *(Enter name and address of paying officer designated by the agreement)* _____
and deemed a "designated pool contract" for the purpose of said Agreement. If this SFRC contract is awarded by one of the other military departments or the Defense Logistics Agency, it will be deemed a "pool contract" for the purpose of said Agreement and, notwithstanding other provisions of this SFRC, all payments hereunder will be by check drawn payable to the dual payee, "Department of the *(Enter name)* _____ or *(Enter name of contractor)* _____ " and forwarded to *(Enter name and address of paying office designated by the Agreement.)* _____
_____ for appropriate disposition.

DD Form 2222-2, 84 APR

Exhibit 28. DOD Short Form Research Contract (cont.).

REPRESENTATIONS AND CERTIFICATIONS FROM OFFERORS
SUBMITTING PROPOSALS UNDER DFARS 35.70

1. CONTINGENT FEE REPRESENTATION AND AGREEMENT (APR 1984) (FAR 52.203-4)

a. REPRESENTATION. The offeror represents that, except for full-time bona fide employees working solely for the offeror, the offeror (X one)

☐ (1) has ☐ (2) has not employed or retained any person or company to solicit or obtain this contract; and (X one)

☐ (3) has ☐ (4) has not paid or agreed to pay to any person or company employed or retained to solicit or obtain this contract any commission, percentage, brokerage, or other fee contingent upon or resulting from the award of this contract.

b. AGREEMENT. The offeror agrees to provide information relating to the above Representation as requested by the Contracting Officer and, when subparagraph 1a above is answered affirmatively, to promptly submit to the Contracting Officer

(1) A completed Standard Form 119, Statement of Contingent or Other Fees, (SF 119); or

(2) A signed statement indicating that SF 119 was previously submitted to the same contracting office, including the date and applicable solicitation or contract number, and representing that the prior SF 119 applies to this offer or quotation.

2. CERTIFICATION OF NONSEGREGATED FACILITIES (APR 1984) (FAR 52.222-21)

a. The offeror (X one)

☐ (1) does ☐ (2) does not maintain or provide to its employees any segregated facilities, and (X one)

☐ (3) will ☐ (4) will not permit any of its employees to perform their service at any location under its control where segregated facilities are maintained. It is agreed that a breach of this certification is a violation of the Equal Opportunity clause in this contract. It is further agreed that identical certificates will be obtained from proposed subcontractors prior to the award of subcontracts exceeding $10,000 which are not exempt from the provision of the Equal Opportunity clause; that such certifications will be maintained in the Offeror's files; and that the notice required by FAR 52.222-21(c) (3) will be forwarded to such proposed subcontractors.

3. PREVIOUS CONTRACTS AND COMPLIANCE REPORTS (APR 1984) (FAR 52.222-22)

a. The offeror (X one)

☐ (1) has ☐ (2) has not participated in a previous contract or subcontract subject either to the Equal Opportunity clause listed in FAR 52.222-26, the clause originally contained in Section 310 of Executive Order No. 10925, or the clause contained in Section 201 of Executive Order No. 11114.

b. The offeror (X one)

☐ (1) has ☐ (2) has not filed all compliance reports. Representations indicating submission of required compliance reports, signed by proposed subcontractors, will be obtained before subcontract awards.

4. AFFIRMATIVE ACTION COMPLIANCE (APR 1984) (FAR 52.222-25)

a. The offeror represents that it (X one)

☐ (1) has developed and has on file or

☐ (2) has not developed and does not have on file at each establishment, affirmative action programs required by the rules and regulations of the Secretary of Labor (41 CFR 60-1 and 60-2), or

☐ (3) has not previously had contracts subject to the written affirmative action programs requirement of the rules and regulations of the Secretary of Labor.

DD Form 2222-1, 84 APR   Previous editions are obsolete.

Exhibit 28. DOD Short Form Research Contract (cont.).

---

5. ORGANIZATIONAL CONFLICTS OF INTEREST (FAR 15.505 (c6) *(X one)*

☐ a. There are no known organizational conflicts of interest.

☐ b. Information is provided as an appendix concerning potential or real organizational conflict of interest.

---

6. CLEAN AIR AND WATER CERTIFICATION (APR 1984) (FAR 52.223-1)

a. The offeror certifies that:

(1) Any facility to be used in the performance of this proposed contract *(X one)*

☐ (a) is   ☐ (b) is not   listed on the Environmental Protection Agency List of Violating Facilities;

(2) The offeror will immediately notify the Contracting Officer, before award, of the receipt of any communication from the Administrator, or a designee, of the Environmental Protection Agency, indicating that any facility that the Offeror proposes to use for the performance of the contract is under consideration to be listed on the EPA List of Violating Facilities; and

(3) The offeror will include a certification substantially the same as this certification, including this paragraph (6a(3)), in every nonexempt subcontract.

---

7. INSURANCE - IMMUNITY FROM TORT LIABILITY (APR 1984) (FAR 52.228-7)

a. The offeror *(X one)*

☐ (1) does   ☐ (2) does not   claim immunity to tort liability as a state or charity institution under

(X one)

☐ (a) Alternate I   ☐ (b) Alternate II

---

8. OFFEROR INFORMATION

a. TYPED NAME OF COMPANY	b. TYPED NAME OF COMPANY REPRESENTATIVE
c. SIGNATURE OF COMPANY REPRESENTATIVE	d. DATE SIGNED *(YYMMDD)*

DD Form 2222-1, 84 APR

Exhibit 28. DOD Short Form Research Contract (cont.).

SUPPLEMENT TO DD FORM 2222-1
REPRESENTATIONS AND CERTIFICATIONS

1. PLACE OF PERFORMANCE   FAR 52.215.20 (APR 1984)

   a. **Representation.** The offeror, in the performance resulting from this solicitation, / / intends, / / does not intend (check applicable block) to use one or more plants or facilities located at a different address from the address of the offeror as indicated in this proposal.

   b. **Definitions.**

If the offeror check "intends" in paragraph (a) above, it shall insert in the spaces provided below the required information:

Place of Performance (Street, Address, City, County, State, Zip Code)	Name and Address of Owner and Operator of the Plant or Facility if Other than Offeror

2. DEBARMENT AND SUSPENSION CERTIFICATE

The Bidder/Offeror, by submission of a bid or offer or execution of a contract in response to this solicitation, certifies that the Bidder/Offeror is not debarred, suspended, declared ineligible for awards of public contracts, or proposed for debarment pursuant to FAR 9.406.2. If the Bidder/Offeror cannot so certify, or if the status of the Bidder/Offeror changes prior to award, then the Bidder/Offeror must provide detailed information as to its current status.

_____   By: _____

(Contractor)   (Signature)

_____   _____

(Date)   (Typed Name & Title)

C. DEPARTMENT OF EDUCATION (ED)

General

The government has made some attempts toward application form standardization. The result has been standard form 424 prescribed by the GSA in Federal Management

Circular 74-8. The Department of Education uses this form entitled "Federal Assistance" in all its programs.

Exhibit 29. ED Federal Assistance Form.

OMB Approval No. 0348-0006	

FEDERAL ASSISTANCE

1. TYPE OF SUBMISSION (Mark appropriate box)
- ☐ NOTICE OF INTENT (OPTIONAL)
- ☐ PREAPPLICATION
- ☒ APPLICATION

2. APPLICANT'S APPLICATION IDENTIFIER
a. NUMBER
b. DATE Year month day 19

Leave Blank

3. STATE APPLICATION IDENTIFIER NOTE: TO BE ASSIGNED BY STATE
a. NUMBER
b. DATE ASSIGNED Year month day 19

4. LEGAL APPLICANT/RECIPIENT
a. Applicant Name
b. Organization Unit
c. Street/P.O. Box
d. City
e. County
f. State
g. ZIP Code.
h. Contact Person (Name & Telephone No.)

5. EMPLOYER IDENTIFICATION NUMBER (EIN)

6. PROGRAM (From CFDA)
a. NUMBER 8 4 ° 1 1 7 E
MULTIPLE ☐
b. TITLE **Field-Initiated Studies**

7. TITLE OF APPLICANT'S PROJECT (Use section IV of this form to provide a summary description of the project.)

8. TYPE OF APPLICANT/RECIPIENT
A—State
B—Interstate
C—Substate Organization
D—County
E—City
F—School District
G—Special Purpose District
H—Community Action Agency
I—Higher Educational Institution
J—Indian Tribe
K—Other (Specify):
Enter appropriate letter ☐

9. AREA OF PROJECT IMPACT (Names of cities, counties, states, etc.)

10. ESTIMATED NUMBER OF PERSONS BENEFITING N.A.

11. TYPE OF ASSISTANCE
A—Basic Grant
B—Supplemental Grant
C—Loan
D—Insurance
E—Other
Enter appropriate letter(s) ☐ A

12. PROPOSED FUNDING
a. FEDERAL	$ .00
b. APPLICANT	N.A. .00
c. STATE	N.A. .00
d. LOCAL	N.A. .00
e. OTHER	N.A. .00
f. Total	$ .00

13. CONGRESSIONAL DISTRICTS OF:
a. APPLICANT
b. PROJECT

15. PROJECT START DATE Year month day 19

16. PROJECT DURATION Months

18. DATE DUE TO FEDERAL AGENCY ▶ 19 88 05 13 Year month day

14. TYPE OF APPLICATION
A—New
B—Renewal
C—Revision
D—Continuation
E—Augmentation
Enter appropriate letter ☐ A

17. TYPE OF CHANGE (For 14c or 14e)
A—Increase Dollars
B—Decrease Dollars
C—Increase Duration
D—Decrease Duration
E—Cancellation
F—Other (Specify):
Enter appropriate letter(s) ☐ ☐ ☐

19. FEDERAL AGENCY TO RECEIVE REQUEST **U.S. Department of Education**
a. ORGANIZATIONAL UNIT (IF APPROPRIATE) **Application Control Center**
b. ADMINISTRATIVE CONTACT (IF KNOWN)
c. ADDRESS **Washington, D.C. 20202**

20. EXISTING FEDERAL GRANT IDENTIFICATION NUMBER N.A.

21. REMARKS ADDED ☐ Yes ☐ No

22. THE APPLICANT CERTIFIES THAT ▶ To the best of my knowledge and belief, data in this preapplication/application are true and correct, the document has been duly authorized by the governing body of the applicant and the applicant will comply with the attached assurances if the assistance is approved.

a. YES, THIS NOTICE OF INTENT/PREAPPLICATION/APPLICATION WAS MADE AVAILABLE TO THE STATE EXECUTIVE ORDER 12372 PROCESS FOR REVIEW ON: DATE _____

b. NO, PROGRAM IS NOT COVERED BY E.O. 12372 ☐ OR PROGRAM HAS NOT BEEN SELECTED BY STATE FOR REVIEW ☐

23. CERTIFYING REPRESENTATIVE
a. TYPED NAME AND TITLE
b. SIGNATURE

24. APPLICATION RECEIVED Year month day 19

25. FEDERAL APPLICATION IDENTIFICATION NUMBER

26. FEDERAL GRANT IDENTIFICATION

27. ACTION TAKEN
- ☐ a. AWARDED
- ☐ b. REJECTED
- ☐ c. RETURNED FOR AMENDMENT
- ☐ d. RETURNED FOR E.O. 12372 SUBMISSION BY APPLICANT TO STATE
- ☐ e. DEFERRED
- ☐ f. WITHDRAWN

28. FUNDING
a. FEDERAL	$ .00
b. APPLICANT	.00
c. STATE	.00
d. LOCAL	.00
e. OTHER	.00
f. TOTAL	$ .00

29. ACTION DATE ▶ Year month day 19

31. CONTACT FOR ADDITIONAL INFORMATION (Name and telephone number)

30. STARTING DATE Year month date 19

32. ENDING DATE Year month date 19

33. REMARKS ADDED ☐ Yes ☐ No

SECTION I—APPLICANT/RECIPIENT DATA
SECTION II—CERTIFICATION
SECTION III—FEDERAL AGENCY ACTION

NSN 7540-01-008-8162
PREVIOUS EDITION IS NOT USABLE

424-103

STANDARD FORM 424 PAGE 1 (Rev. 4-84)
Prescribed by OMB Circular A-102

Institutional Information Required

Along with the standard project information, there are several items of information needed to complete the application forms that may not be readily accessible. Therefore, you should have them in advance to make completion of the forms easier. These are:

1. Congressional district;
2. Federal Employer Identification No. (IRS #);
3. Type of organization of applicant (list provided—select one);
4. Estimated number of persons benefiting from the assistance;
5. Sources of funding for project.

Project Questions

If the project is subject to a State Clearinghouse submission pursuant to the OMB Circular A-95, the responses must be attached to the application.

Exhibit 30. Financial Status Report.

FINANCIAL STATUS REPORT				
(Short Form)				
(Follow instructions on the back)				

1. Federal Agency and Organizational Element to Which Report is Submitted	2. Federal Grant or Other Identifying Number Assigned By Federal Agency	OMB Approval No. **0348-0039**	Page	of pages

3. Recipient Organization (Name and complete address, including ZIP code)

4. Employer Identification Number	5. Recipient Account Number or Identifying Number	6. Final Report ☐ Yes ☐ No	7. Basis ☐ Cash ☐ Accrual

8. Funding/Grant Period (See *Instructions*) From: (Month, Day, Year)	To : (Month, Day, Year)	9. Period Covered by this Report From: (Month, Day, Year)	To: (Month, Day, Year)

10. Transactions:	I Previously Reported	II This Period	III Cumulative
a. Total outlays			
b. Recipient share of outlays			
c. Federal share of outlays			
d. Total unliquidated obligations			
e. Recipient share of unliquidated obligations			
f. Federal share of unliquidated obligations			
g. Total Federal share (Sum of lines c and f)			
h. Total Federal funds authorized for this funding period			
i. Unobligated balance of Federal funds (Line h minus line g)			

11. Indirect Expense	a. Type of Rate (Place "X" in appropriate box) ☐ Provisional ☐ Predetermined ☐ Final ☐ Fixed			
	b. Rate	c. Base	d. Total Amount	e. Federal Share

12. Remarks: Attach any explanations deemed necessary or information required by Federal sponsoring agency in compliance with governing legislation.

13. Certification: I certify to the best of my knowledge and belief that this report is correct and complete and that all outlays and unliquidated obligations are for the purposes set forth in the award documents.	
Typed or Printed Name and Title	Telephone (Area code, number and extension)
Signature of Authorized Certifying Official	Date Report Submitted

Previous Editions not Usable

Standard Form 269A (REV 4-88)
Prescribed by OMB Circulars A-102 and A-110

D. DEPARTMENT OF HEALTH AND HUMAN SERVICES (HHS)

General

HHS uses several forms—similar, but different nevertheless. Form PHS 398 (Rev. 10-88) is most familiar as it is used to apply for all new, competing continuation, and supplemental research and training grant and cooperative agreement support except as shown in the Figure below.

Continuation grants by HHS definition are for projects previously funded but whose funding term is finishing, thereby putting it in a "competitive" situation with new proposals. However, if an applicant has the information to complete a PHS 398 application, all the others will be routine. Therefore, discussion will focus on PHS 398.

Institutional Information Required

Along with the standard application and project information there are several items of information needed to complete the application forms that may not be readily accessible. Therefore, you should have them in advance to make completion of the forms easier. These are:

1. Entity Identification # (EIN # assigned by IRS);
2. Name of official in business office to be notified of award;
3. Has the project had clearance by Institutional Review Boards if human subjects or animals are involved in the research?
4. Does the project involve recombinant DNA?

Exhibit 31. Types of HHS Forms.

Forms

Use Form PHS 398 to apply for all new, competing continuation, and supplemental research and research training grant and cooperative agreement support, except as shown in the table below:

Type of Application	Use Form Number
Small Business Innovation Research Program—Phase I	PHS 6246-1
Small Business Innovation Research Program—Phase II	PHS 6246-2
Individual National Research Service Award or Senior International Fellowship Award	PHS 416-1
International Research Fellowship Award	NIH 1541-1
Nonresearch Training Grant	PHS 6025
Grant to State or Local Government Agency	PHS 5161-1
Health Services Project	PHS 5161-1
Construction Grant	NIH 2575
Biomedical Research Support Grant	NIH 147-1

Most of the above application forms have corresponding forms to be used when applying for noncompeting continuation support during an approved project period. The form corresponding to PHS 398 is Form PHS 2590.

Exhibit 32. HHS Grant Application.

Form Approved Through 3/31/91
OMB No. 0925-0001

DEPARTMENT OF HEALTH AND HUMAN SERVICES
PUBLIC HEALTH SERVICE

GRANT APPLICATION

Follow instructions carefully. Type in the unshaded areas only.

LEAVE BLANK FOR PHS USE ONLY.		
Type	Activity	Number
Review Group		Formerly
Council/Board (Month, Year)		Date Received

1. TITLE OF PROJECT (Do not exceed 56 typewriter spaces.)

2. RESPONSE TO SPECIFIC PROGRAM ANNOUNCEMENT ☐ NO ☐ YES (If "YES," state RFA number and/or announcement title)
Number: Title:

3. PRINCIPAL INVESTIGATOR/PROGRAM DIRECTOR   ☐ NEW INVESTIGATOR

3a. NAME (Last, first, middle)	3b. DEGREE(S)	3c. SOCIAL SECURITY NO.

3d. POSITION TITLE   3e. MAILING ADDRESS (Street, city, state, zip code)

3f. DEPARTMENT, SERVICE, LABORATORY, OR EQUIVALENT

3g. MAJOR SUBDIVISION

3h. TELEPHONE (Area code, number, and extension)

4. HUMAN SUBJECTS   IRB   5. VERTEBRATE ANIMALS   If "YES,"   5b. Animal welfare
                    If "YES,"   approval   4b. Assurance of   IACUC approval date   assurance no.
    4a.   exemption no. **or**   date   compliance no.   5a.
    NO   YES   NO   YES

6. DATES OF ENTIRE PROPOSED PROJECT PERIOD	7. COSTS REQUESTED FOR FIRST 12-MONTH BUDGET PERIOD		8. COSTS REQUESTED FOR ENTIRE PROPOSED PROJECT PERIOD	
From (YYMMDD) Through (YYMMDD)	7a. Direct Costs	7b. Total Costs	8a. Direct Costs	8b. Total Costs
	$	$	$	$

9. PERFORMANCE SITES (Organizations and addresses)

10. INVENTIONS (Competing continuation application only)

☐ NO ☐ YES If "YES," ☐ Previously reported ☐ Not previously reported

11. NAME OF APPLICANT ORGANIZATION

ADDRESS (Street, city, state, and zip code)

13. ENTITY IDENTIFICATION NUMBER	Congressional District

12. TYPE OF ORGANIZATON
☐ Public: Specify ☐ Federal ☐ State ☐ Local
☐ Private Nonprofit
☐ For Profit (General) ☐ For Profit (Small Business)

14. ORGANIZATIONAL COMPONENT TO RECEIVE CREDIT TOWARDS A BIOMEDICAL RESEARCH SUPPORT GRANT
Code: Identification:

15. NAME OF OFFICIAL IN BUSINESS OFFICE

TELEPHONE (Area code, number, and extension)

TITLE

ADDRESS

16. NAME OF OFFICIAL SIGNING FOR APPLICANT ORGANIZATION

TELEPHONE (Area code, number, and extension)

TITLE

ADDRESS

17. PRINCIPAL INVESTIGATOR/PROGRAM DIRECTOR ASSURANCE: I agree to accept responsibility for the scientific conduct of the project and to provide the required progress reports if a grant is awarded as a result of this application. Willful provision of false information is a criminal offense (U.S. Code, Title 18, Section 1001).

SIGNATURE OF PERSON NAMED IN 3a
(In ink. "Per" signature not acceptable.)   DATE

18. CERTIFICATION AND ACCEPTANCE: I certify that the statements herein are true and complete to the best of my knowledge, and accept the obligation to comply with Public Health Service terms and conditions if a grant is awarded as the result of this application. A willfully false certification is a criminal offense (U.S. Code, Title 18, Section 1001).

SIGNATURE OF PERSON NAMED IN 16
(In ink. "Per" signature not acceptable)   DATE

PHS 398 (Rev. 10/88) (Reprinted 9/89)   AA

DUPLICATE COPY - USE IF NEEDED

Exhibit 32. HHS Grant Application (cont.).

BB   PRINCIPAL INVESTIGATOR/PROGRAM DIRECTOR: _____

DESCRIPTION: State the application's broad, long-term objectives and specific aims, making reference to the health relatedness of the project. Describe concisely the experimental design and methods for achieving these goals. Avoid summaries of past accomplishments and the use of the first person. This abstract is meant to serve as a succinct and accurate description of the proposed work when separated from the application. **DO NOT EXCEED THE SPACE PROVIDED.**

DUPLICATE COPY - USE IF NEEDED

KEY PERSONNEL ENGAGED ON PROJECT

NAME, DEGREE(S), SSN	POSITION TITLE AND ROLE IN PROJECT	DEPARTMENT AND ORGANIZATION

Exhibit 32. HHS Grant Application (cont.).

CC   PRINCIPAL INVESTIGATOR/PROGRAM DIRECTOR: _____

Type the name of the Principal Investigator/Program Director at the top of each printed page and each continuation page. (For type specifications, see **Specific Instructions** on page 12.)

TABLE OF CONTENTS

SECTION 1.   PAGE NUMBERS

Face Page, Description and Key Personnel, Table of Contents...................................... 1-3
Detailed Budget for First 12-Month Budget Period.. 4
Budget for Entire Proposed Project Period.. 5
Budgets Pertaining to Consortium/Contractual Arrangements.................................. _____
Biographical Sketch-Principal Investigator/Program Director *(Not to exceed two pages)*................ _____
Other Biographical Sketches *(Not to exceed two pages for each)*................................ _____
Other Support.. _____
Resources and Environment.. _____

SECTION 2. Research Plan

Introduction to Revised or Supplemental application *(Not to exceed one page)*..................... _____
A. Specific Aims.................. ⎫
B. Background and Significance ...... ⎪ .... _____
C. Progress Report/Preliminary Studies ⎬ *(Not to exceed 20 pages*)* .... _____
D. Experimental Design and Methods.. ⎭ .... _____
E. Human Subjects.................... _____
F. Vertebrate Animals................ _____
G. Consultants/Collaborators........ _____
H. Consortium/Contractual Arrangements... _____
I. Literature Cited *(Not to exceed four pages)*.. _____
Checklist.. _____

*Type density and pitch must conform to limits provided in **Specific Instructions** on page 12.

SECTION 3. Appendix *(Six collated sets. No page numbering necessary for Appendix)*

Number of publications and manuscripts accepted for publication *(Not to exceed ten)*: _____
Other items (list):

DUPLICATE COPY - USE IF NEEDED

E. NATIONAL ENDOWMENT FOR THE ARTS (NEA)

General

NEA uses several versions of its form (OMB #128-R0001). There is one version for submissions from individuals and one for organizations, also modified slightly by program, i.e., literature or museum. Still, they are all similar. Included here are three sets of forms.

Institutional Information Required

Along with the normal project information, NEA has added the requirement that project budget information be included in the application form. Therefore, the institution representative must be prepared to understand the budget completely to ensure the line items are completed correctly. The budgets include requests not only for information on expenditures, but also contributions, revenues, and grants that might be relevant to the project. They then ask that the institutional authorizing official sign a statement that the information is true and correct to the best of his/her knowledge.

Project Questions

As a last bit of information, the application requires completion of an assurance that the applicant institution will comply with Title VI of the Civil Rights Act of 1964, Section 504 of the Rehabilitation Act of 1973, and Title IX of the Education Amendments of 1972. These are standard compliances but the institutional application preparer should be familiar with what will be required if the grant is received. This is particularly important in view of legislation and regulations placing restrictions on NEA funded projects.

Exhibit 33. NEA Individual Grant Application Form—Literature.

OMB No. 3135-0049 Expires 9/30/91 47

Literature Program Fiscal Year 1992	**Individual Grant Application Form NEA-2 (Rev.)** This application form must be submitted in triplicate together with other required materials and mailed to: Information Management Division/LIT FEL, 8th floor, National Endowment for the Arts, Nancy Hanks Center, 1100 Pennsylvania Avenue, N.W., Washington, D.C. 20506

1. Name (last, first, middle initial)

4. Literature Program Fellowships
Check one:
☐ Fiction
☐ Poetry
☐ Creative Non-Fiction
☐ Translation   Specify Language: _____
☐ Collaboration

2. Permanent mailing address/phone

5. U.S. Citizenship

☐ Yes   ☐ No   (Visa Number: _____)

6. Professional field or discipline:

3. Present mailing address/phone

7.
_____
Birthdate

_____
Place of birth

___ — ___
Social Security Number

8. Period of support requested
Starting
_____
       month   day   year

Ending
_____
       month   day   year

9. Fellowship for Creative Writer: Amount requested: $20,000. No project description necessary.

10. Translators: Amount requested (circle one): $10,000 $20,000
Description of proposed activity

11. Summary of Publications (Use this space to document your eligibility.) You may attach one additional sheet if necessary.

Titles	Name of Magazine or Press (include address and phone number)	Publication Dates

(Continued on reverse)

Exhibit 33. NEA Individual Grant Application Form—Literature (cont.).

11. Summary of publications (continued)

2

12. Education

Name of Institution	Major area of study	Inclusive dates	Degree

13. Fellowships or grants previously awarded

Name of award	Area of study	Inclusive dates	Amount

14. Present employment

Employer	Position/Occupation

15. Prizes/Honors received   **Membership/professional societies**

16. Final Reports

Have you submitted required Final Report packages on all completed Arts Endowment grants since (and including) Fiscal Year 1984?

_____ Yes _____ No   If no, please mail immediately, under separate cover, to Grants Office/Final Reports Section to maintain eligibility. <u>Do not include with your application package.</u>

17. Delinquent Debt

Are you delinquent on repayment of any Federal debt (e.g. student loans, delinquent taxes)? _____ Yes _____ No. If yes, provide explanatory information on a separate sheet.

18. Certification: I certify that the foregoing statements are true and complete to the best of my knowledge. I also certify that, in compliance with the Drug-Free Workplace Act of 1988, I will not engage in the unlawful manufacture, distribution, dispensation, possession, or use of a controlled substance in conducting any activity with the grant.

x_____   _____
   Signature of applicant   Date

BE SURE TO DOUBLE CHECK THE "HOW TO APPLY" SECTION ON PAGE 43. AND, IF APPLICABLE, THE SPECIAL APPLICATION REQUIREMENTS FOR YOUR CATEGORY FOR ALL MATERIALS TO BE INCLUDED IN YOUR APPLICATION PACKAGE. LATE APPLICATIONS WILL BE REJECTED. INCOMPLETE APPLICATIONS ARE UNLIKELY TO BE FUNDED.

Privacy Act

The Privacy Act of 1974 requires us to furnish you with the following information:

The Endowment is authorized to solicit the requested information by Section 5 of the National Foundation on the Arts and the Humanities Act of 1965, as amended. The information is used for grant processing, statistical research, analysis of trends, and for congressional oversight hearings. Failure to provide the requested information could result in rejection of your application.

Exhibit 34. NEA Organization Grant Application Form—Literature.

OMB No. 3135-0049 Expires 9/30/91   49

| Literature Program Fiscal Year 1992 | **Organization Grant Application Form NEA-3 (Rev.)** Applications must be submitted in triplicate together with other required materials and mailed to: Information Management Division/LIT, 8th floor, National Endowment for the Arts, Nancy Hanks Center, 1100 Pennsylvania Avenue, N.W., Washington, D.C. 20506 |

I. Applicant organization (name, address, zip)

II. Category under which support is requested:

☐ Literary Publishing
_____ Literary Magazines
_____ Small Presses
_____ Distribution Projects

☐ Audience Development
_____ Residencies for Writers and Reading Series
_____ Literary Centers
_____ Audience Development Projects

☐ Professional Development

III. Period of support requested:

Starting _____
     month   day   year
Ending _____
     month   day   year

IV. Employer Identification Number: _____

V. Summary of project description. Specify clearly how the requested funds will be spent. (Complete in space provided unless "Application Requirements" for your category specify otherwise).

VI. Estimated number of persons expected to benefit from this project

VII. Summary of estimated costs (recapitulation of budget items in Section X)   **Total costs of activity**

A.   **Direct costs**
     Salaries and wages $ _____
     Fringe benefits
     Supplies and materials
     Travel
     Permanent equipment
     Fees and other
                   Total direct costs $ _____
B.   **Indirect costs** $ _____
                   Total project costs $ _____
                  (rounded to nearest $10)

VIII. Total amount requested from the National Endowment for the Arts $ _____

    NOTE: This amount (amount requested): $ _____
    PLUS Total contributions, grants, and revenues (XI., page 3): + _____
    MUST EQUAL Total project costs (VII. above): = _____

IX. Organization total fiscal activity	Most recently completed fiscal year	Estimated for fiscal year related to grant
A. Expenses	1. $ _____	2. $ _____
B. Contributions, grants, & revenues	1. $ _____	2. $ _____

Do not write in this space

PYS: $

Exhibit 34. NEA Organization Grant Application Form—Literature (cont.).

X. Budget breakdown of summary of estimated costs

    A. Direct costs

        1. Salaries and wages

Title and/or type of personnel	Number of personnel	Annual or average salary range	% of time devoted to this project	Amount $

Total salaries and wages $ _____
Add fringe benefits $ _____
Total salaries and wages including fringe benefits $ _____

        2. Supplies and materials (list each major type separately)

	Amount $

Total supplies and material $ _____

        3. Travel

Transportation of personnel

No. of travelers	from	to	Amount $

Total transportation of personnel $ _____

Subsistence

No. of travelers	No. of days	Daily rate	$

Total subsistence $ _____
Total travel $ _____

Exhibit 34. NEA Organization Grant Application Form—Literature (cont.).

X. Budget breakdown of summary of estimated costs (continued)

3

    4. Permanent equipment

Amount
$

Total permanent equipment $ _____

    5. Fees for services and other expenses (list each item separately)

Amount
$

Total fees and other $ _____

B. Indirect costs

Amount

Rate established by attached negotiation agreement with
National Endowment for the Arts or another Federal agency
Rate _____ % Base _____

$ _____

XI. Contributions, grants, and revenues (for this project)

  A. Contributions

Amount

    1. Cash

$ _____

    2. In-kind contributions (list each major item)

Total contributions $ _____

  B. Grants (do not list anticipated grant from the Arts Endowment)

Total grants $ _____

  C. Revenues

Total revenues $ _____
Total contributions, grants, and revenues for this project $ _____

Exhibit 34. NEA Organization Grant Application Form—Literature (cont.).

XII. Final Reports 4

Have you submitted required Final Report packages on all completed grants
<u>from any Arts Endowment Program</u> since (and including) Fiscal Year 1984? (i.e., any grant letter dated on or after October 1, 1983)

_____ Yes _____ No   If no, please mail immediately, under separate cover, to Grants Office/Final Reports Section
to maintain eligibility. <u>Do not include with your application package.</u>

XIII. Delinquent Debt

Are you delinquent on repayment of any Federal debt? _____ Yes _____ No
If yes, provide explanatory information on a separate sheet.

XIV. Certification

The Authorizing Official(s) certify that the information contained in this application, including all attachments and supporting
materials, is true and correct to the best of our knowledge. The Authorizing Official(s) also certify that the applicant will comply
with the Federal requirements specified under "Assurance of Compliance" on pages 39-42.

<u>Authorizing Official(s)</u>

Signature   X _____ Date signed _____
Name (print or type)   _____
Title (print or type)   _____
Telephone (area code)   _____

Signature   X _____ Date signed _____
Name (print or type)   _____
Title (print or type)   _____
Telephone (area code)   _____

<u>Project director</u>

Signature   X _____ Date signed _____
Name (print or type)   _____
Title (print or type)   _____
Telephone (area code)   _____

*Payee (to whom grant payments will be sent if other than authorizing official)

Signature   X _____ Date signed _____
Name (print or type)   _____
Title (print or type)   _____
Telephone (area code)   _____

*If payment is to be made to anyone other than the grantee, it is understood that the grantee is financially, administratively, and
programmatically responsible for all aspects of the grant and that all reports must be submitted through the grantee.

BE SURE TO DOUBLE CHECK THE "HOW TO APPLY" SECTION ON PAGE 43 AND THE APPLICATION PACKAGE.

LATE APPLICATIONS WILL BE REJECTED.

INCOMPLETE APPLICATIONS ARE UNLIKELY TO BE FUNDED.

Privacy Act

The Privacy Act of 1974 requires us to furnish you with the following information:

The Endowment is authorized to solicit the requested information by Section 5 of the National
Foundation on the Arts and the Humanities Act of 1965, as amended. The information is used for
grant processing, statistical research, analysis of trends, and for congressional oversight hearings.
Failure to provide the requested information could result in rejection of your application.

Exhibit 35. NEA Organization Grant Application Form—Museum.

47

3

X. Budget breakdown of summary of estimated costs (continued)

4. Permanent equipment ($5,000 or more per unit)   Amount
$

Total permanent equipment $ _____

5. Fees for services and other expenses (list each item separately) $

Total fees and other $ _____

B. Indirect costs   Amount

Rate established by attached rate negotiation agreement with
National Endowment for the Arts or another Federal agency
Rate _____ % Base _____ Negotiated with _____ $ _____

XI. Contributions, grants, and revenues (for this project)

A. Contributions   Amount

1. Cash $

Total cash $ _____

2. In-kind contributions (list each major item)

Total contributions $ _____

B. Grants (do not list anticipated grant from the Arts Endowment)

Total grants $ _____

C. Revenues

Total revenues $ _____
Total contributions, grants, and revenues for this project $ _____

(Continued on reverse)

Exhibit 35. NEA Organization Grant Application Form—Museum (cont.).

OMB No. 3135-0053 Expires 8/31/92   45

Museum Fiscal Year 1992	Organization Grant Application Form NEA-3 (Rev.)
	Applications must be submitted in triplicate and mailed together with other required materials to: Information Management Division/MM, 8th floor, National Endowment for the Arts, Nancy Hanks Center, 1100 Pennsylvania Avenue, N.W., Washington, D.C. 20506 (overnight mail zip code: 20004)

I. Applicant Organization: IRS name (popular name, if different), address, zip	II. Category under which support is requested:	III. Period of support requested: Starting _____ month day year Ending _____ month day year
		IV. Employer I.D. number:

V. Summary of project activity: (Complete in space provided. DO NOT reduce copy or continue on additional pages.)

VI. Estimated number of persons expected to benefit from this activity:

VII. Summary of estimated costs: (recapitulation of budget items in Section X)

    A. Direct costs   **Total costs of project**

Salaries and wages	_____	$ _____
Fringe benefits	_____	$ _____
Supplies and materials	_____	$ _____
Travel	_____	$ _____
Permanent equipment	_____	$ _____
Fees and other	_____	$ _____
	Total direct costs	$ _____
B. Indirect costs	_____	$ _____
	Total project costs	$ _____
	(rounded to nearest hundred dollars)	

VIII. Total amount requested from the National Endowment for the Arts : . . . . $ _____

    NOTE: Amount requested from Arts Endowment (VIII.): $ _____
    PLUS Total contributions, grants, and revenues (XI., page 3):   + _____
    MUST EQUAL Total project costs (VII. above):   = _____

IX. Organization total fiscal activity:

	Most recently completed fiscal year	Estimated for fiscal year relating to grant period
A. Expenses	1. $ _____	2. $ _____
B. Contributions, grants, and revenues	1. $ _____	2. $ _____

(Continued on reverse)

Exhibit 35. NEA Organization Grant Application Form—Museum (cont.).

X. Budget breakdown of summary of estimated costs   2

   A. Direct costs

      1. Salaries and wages

Title and/or type of personnel	Number of personnel	Annual or average salary range exclusive of incidentals	% of time devoted to this project	Amount $

Total salaries and wages $ _____

Add fringe benefits $ _____

Total salaries and wages including fringe benefits $ _____

2. Supplies and materials (list each major type separately)   Amount $

Total supplies and materials $ _____

3. Travel

Transportation of personnel   Amount

No. of travelers	from	to	$

Total transportation of personnel $ _____

Subsistence

No. of travelers	No. of days	Daily rate	$

Total subsistence $ _____

Total travel $ _____

(Continued on next page)

Exhibit 35. NEA Organization Grant Application Form—Museum (cont.).

48

XII. To what other Federal funding sources (including other Arts Endowment programs) have you applied since October 1, 1990, **4** or do you intend to apply this year or next, for support of this project or program? _____

XIII. **Final Reports**

Have you submitted required Final Report packages on all completed Arts Endowment grants since (and including) Fiscal Year 1984?

_____ Yes _____ No   If no, please mail immediately, under separate cover, to Grants Office / Final Reports Section to maintain eligibility. Do <u>not</u> include with your application package.

XIV. **Delinquent Debt**

Are you delinquent on repayment of any Federal debt? _____ Yes _____ No.
If yes, provide explanatory information on a separate sheet.

XV. **Certification**

The Authorizing Official(s) certify that the information contained in this application, including all attachments and supporting materials, is true and correct to the best of our knowledge. The Authorizing Official(s) also certify that the applicant will comply with the Federal requirements specified under "Assurance of Compliance" on pages 37-39.

<u>Authorizing Official(s)</u>

Signature   X _____   Date signed _____
Name (print or type)   _____
Title (print or type)   _____
Telephone (area code)   _____

Signature   X _____   Date signed _____
Name (print or type)   _____
Title (print or type)   _____
Telephone (area code)   _____

<u>Project director</u>

Signature   X _____   Date signed _____
Name (print or type)   _____
Title (print or type)   _____
Telephone (area code)   _____

*<u>Payee</u> (to whom grant payments will be sent if other than authorizing official)

Signature   X _____   Date signed _____
Name (print or type)   _____
Title (print or type)   _____
Telephone (area code)   _____

*If payment is to be made to anyone other than the <u>grantee</u>, it is understood that the <u>grantee</u> is financially, administratively, and programmatically responsible for all aspects of the grant and that all reports must be submitted through the grantee.

BE SURE TO DOUBLE CHECK THE "SUBMITTING YOUR APPLICATION" SECTION ON PAGE 41 AND "SPECIAL APPLICATION REQUIREMENTS" SECTION UNDER THE APPROPRIATE CATEGORY FOR ALL MATERIALS TO BE INCLUDED IN YOUR APPLICATION PACKAGE. LATE APPLICATIONS WILL BE REJECTED. INCOMPLETE APPLICATIONS ARE UNLIKELY TO BE FUNDED.

Privacy Act

The Privacy Act of 1974 requires us to furnish you with the following information:

The Endowment is authorized to solicit the requested information by Section 5 of the National Foundation on the Arts and the Humanities Act of 1965, as amended. The information is used for grant processing, statistical research, analysis of trends, and for congressional oversight hearings. Failure to provide the requested information could result in rejection of your application.

F. NATIONAL ENDOWMENT FOR THE HUMANITIES (NEH)

General

NEH uses the same application form for all programs (form OMB# 3136.0059 exp. 6/30/90)

Institutional Information Required

NEH requires some minimal budget information on its applications form, certainly to a lesser degree of detail than NEA, but nevertheless requiring a knowledge of where the *total* resources for the project will come from. In addition, the application form requests information on the direct beneficiaries of the program and the institution's congressional district.

Project Questions

The application asks if the project has been submitted to another NEH program, another government agency, or a private entity.

Exhibit 36. NEH Grant Application Form.

NEH APPLICATION COVER SHEET

OMB No. 3136-0059
Expires 6/30/92

1. Individual applicant or project director
a. Name and mailing address

Name _____
       (last)   (first)   (initial)

Address _____

_____

_____
  (city)   (state)   (zip code)

b. Form of address: ☐

c. Social Security # _n/a_ Date of birth _n/a_
                          (mo./day/yr.)

d. Telephone number
Office: _____/_____ Home: _____/_____
    (area code)   (area code)

e. Major field of applicant or project director _____ ☐ (code)

f. Citizenship ☐ U.S.
           ☐ Other _____
                  (specify)

2. Type of applicant
a. ☐ by an individual **b.** ☐ through an org./institute
If a, indicate an institutional affiliation, if applicable, on line 11a.
If b, complete block 11 below and indicate here:
c. Type
d. Status

3. Type of application
a. ☐ new   **c.** ☐ renewal
b. ☐ revision and resubmission   **d.** ☐ supplement
If either c or d, indicate previous grant number:
_____

4. Program to which application is being made ☐

_____
Endowment Initiatives: _____
                  (code)

5. Requested grant period
From: _____ To: _____
    (month/year)   (month/year)

6. Project funding
a. Outright funds $ _____
b. Federal match $ _____
c. Total from NEH $ _____
d. Cost sharing $ _____
e. Total project costs $ _____

7. Field of project ☐

8. Descriptive title of project

9. Description of project (do not exceed space provided)

10. Will this proposal be submitted to another government agency or private entity for funding?
(if yes, indicate where and when):
_____

11. Institutional data
a. Institution or organization: _____ _____ _____
                           (name)   (city)   (state)
b. Name of authorizing official: _____ . _____ _____
                             (last)   (first)   (initial)
    Title: _____ Signature: _____ Date _____
c. Institutional grant administrator—name and mailing address:
_____ _____ _____
(last)   (first)   (initial)

Form of address ☐

_____

Telephone: _____/_____
          (area code)
_____ _____ _____
(city)   (state)   (zip code)

12. Student loan status
Is the individual applicant or project director currently delinquent on repayments of any federally backed student loans?
Note: Knowingly providing false information may subject the applicant to criminal penalties of up to $10,000 or imprisonment of up to five years, or both. 18 U.S.C. §1001.

Not applicable

For NEH use only
Date received
Application #
Initials

Exhibit 36. NEH Grant Application Form (cont.).

National Endowment for the Humanities
BUDGET INSTRUCTIONS

Before developing a project budget, applicants should review those sections of the program guidelines and application instructions that discuss cost-sharing requirements, the different kinds of Endowment funding, limitations on the length of the grant period, and any restrictions on the types of costs that may appear in the project budget.

Requested Grant Period

Grant periods begin on the first day of the month and end on the last day of the month. All project activities must take place during the requested grant period.

Project Costs

The budget should include the project costs that will be charged to grant funds as well as those that will be supported by applicant or third-party cash and in-kind contributions.

All of the items listed, whether supported by grant funds or cost-sharing contributions, must be reasonable, necessary to accomplish project objectives, allowable in terms of the applicable federal cost principles, auditable, and incurred during the grant period. Charges to the project for items such as salaries, fringe benefits, travel, and contractual services must conform to the written policies and established practices of the applicant organization.

When indirect costs are charged to the project, care should be taken that expenses that are included in the organization's indirect cost pool (see Indirect Costs) are not charged to the project as direct costs.

Fringe Benefits

Fringe benefits may include contributions for social security, employee insurance, pension plans, etc. Only those benefits that are not included in an organization's indirect cost pool may be shown as direct costs.

Travel Costs

Less-than-first-class accommodations must be used and foreign travel must be undertaken on U.S. flag carriers when such services are available.

Equipment

Only when an applicant can demonstrate that the purchase of permanent equipment will be less expensive than rental may charges be made to the project for such purchases. Permanent equipment is defined as an item costing more than $500 with an estimated useful life of more than two years.

Indirect Costs (Overhead)

These are costs that are incurred for common or joint objectives and therefore cannot be readily identified with a specific project or activity of an organization. Typical examples of indirect cost type items are the salaries of executive officers, the costs of operating and maintaining facilities, local telephone service, office supplies, and accounting and legal services.

Indirect costs are computed by applying a negotiated indirect cost rate to a distribution base (usually the direct costs of the project). Organizations that wish to include overhead charges in the budget but do not have a current federally negotiated indirect cost rate or have not submitted a pending indirect cost proposal to a federal agency may choose one of the following options:

1. The Endowment will not require the formal negotiation of an indirect cost rate, provided the charge for indirect costs does not exceed 10 percent of direct costs, less distorting items (e.g., capital expenditures, major subcontracts), up to a maximum charge of $5,000. (Applicants who choose this option should understand that they must maintain documentation to support overhead charges claimed as part of project costs.)

2. If your organization wishes to use a rate higher than 10 percent or claim more than $5,000 in indirect costs, an estimate of the indirect cost rate and the charges should be provided on the budget form. If the application is approved for funding, you will be instructed to contact the NEH Audit Office to develop an indirect cost proposal.

SAMPLE BUDGET COMPUTATIONS

						NEH Funds (a)	Cost Sharing (b)	Total (c)
Salaries and Wages								
Jane Doe/Project Director	[ ]	9 months x 100% @ $27,000/academic yr.				$13,500	$13,500	$27,000
Jane Doe	[ ]	1 summer month x 100% @ $3,000				3,000		3,000
John Smith/Research Assistant	[ ]	6 months x 50% @ $25,000/yr.				6,250		6,250
Secretarial Support	[1]	3 months x 100% @ $14,000/yr.				3,500		3,500
Fringe Benefits								
11 % of $36,250						2,503	1,485	3,988
8 % of $ 3,500						280		280
	no. of persons	total travel days	subsistence costs	transport. costs =				
Travel								
New York City/Chicago	[2]	[4]	$300	$430		730		730
Various/Washington D.C. conf.	[5]	[10]	$750	500		1,250		1,250
Consultant Fees								
Serbo-Croatian Specialist		5	$100			500		500
Services								
Long Distance Telephone	est. 40 toll calls @ $3.00					120		120
Conference Brochure	50 copies @ $3.50/copy					175		175
TOTAL DIRECT COSTS						$31,808	$14,985	$46,793
Indirect Costs								
20% of $46,793						$ 6,362	$ 2,997	$ 9,359
TOTAL PROJECT COSTS (Direct and Indirect)						$38,170	$17,982	$56,152

Exhibit 36. NEH Grant Application Form (cont.).

National Endowment for the Humanities

OMB No. 3136-0071

BUDGET FORM

Project Director	If this is a revised budget, indicate the NEH application/grant number:
Applicant Organization	Requested Grant Period From _____ to _____ mo/yr · mo/yr

The three-column budget has been developed for the convenience of those applicants who wish to identify the project costs that will be charged to NEH funds and those that will be cost shared. FOR NEH PURPOSES, THE ONLY COLUMN THAT NEEDS TO BE COMPLETED IS COLUMN C. The method of cost computation should clearly indicate how the total charge for each budget item was determined. If more space is needed for any budget category, please follow the budget format on a separate sheet of paper.

When the requested grant period is eighteen months or longer, separate budgets for each twelve-month period of the project must be developed on duplicated copies of the budget form.

SECTION A — budget detail for the period from _____ to _____
mo/yr · mo/yr

1. Salaries and Wages

Provide the names and titles of principal project personnel. For support staff, include the title of each position and indicate in brackets the number of persons who will be employed in that capacity. For persons employed on an academic year basis, list separately any salary charge for work done outside the academic year.

name/title of position	no.	method of cost computation (see sample)	NEH Funds (a)	Cost Sharing (b)	Total (c)
_____	[ ]	_____	$_____	$_____	$_____
_____	[ ]	_____	_____	_____	_____
_____	[ ]	_____	_____	_____	_____
_____	[ ]	_____	_____	_____	_____
_____	[ ]	_____	_____	_____	_____
_____	[ ]	_____	_____	_____	_____
_____	[ ]	_____	_____	_____	_____
_____	[ ]	_____	_____	_____	_____
		SUBTOTAL	$_____	$_____	$_____

2. Fringe Benefits

If more than one rate is used, list each rate and salary base.

rate		salary base	(a)	(b)	(c)
_____ %	of	$_____	$_____	$_____	$_____
_____ %	of	$_____	_____	_____	_____
		SUBTOTAL	$_____	$_____	$_____

3. Consultant Fees

Include payments for professional and technical consultants and honoraria.

name or type of consultant	no. of days on project	daily rate of compensation	(a)	(b)	(c)
_____	_____	$_____	$_____	$_____	$_____
_____	_____	$_____	_____	_____	_____
_____	_____	$_____	_____	_____	_____
_____	_____	$_____	_____	_____	_____
_____	_____	$_____	_____	_____	_____
		SUBTOTAL	$_____	$_____	$_____

Exhibit 36. NEH Grant Application Form (cont.).

4. Travel

For each trip, indicate the number of persons traveling, the total days they will be in travel status, and the total subsistence and transportation costs for that trip. When a project will involve the travel of a number of people to a conference, institute, etc., these costs may be summarized on one line by indicating the point of origin as "various." All foreign travel must be listed separately.

from/to	no. of persons	total travel days	subsistence costs +	transportation costs =	**NEH Funds** (a)	**Cost Sharing** (b)	**Total** (c)
_____	[ ]	[ ]	$_____	$_____	$_____	$_____	$_____
_____	[ ]	[ ]	_____	_____	_____	_____	_____
_____	[ ]	[ ]	_____	_____	_____	_____	_____
_____	[ ]	[ ]	_____	_____	_____	_____	_____
_____	[ ]	[ ]	_____	_____	_____	_____	_____
_____	[ ]	[ ]	_____	_____	_____	_____	_____
_____	[ ]	[ ]	_____	_____	_____	_____	_____
				SUBTOTAL	$_____	$_____	$_____

5. Supplies and Materials

Include consumable supplies, materials to be used in the project, and items of expendable equipment; i.e., equipment items costing less than $500 or with an estimated useful life of less than two years.

item	basis/method of cost computation	(a)	(b)	(c)
_____	_____	$_____	$_____	$_____
_____	_____	_____	_____	_____
_____	_____	_____	_____	_____
_____	_____	_____	_____	_____
_____	_____	_____	_____	_____
_____	_____	_____	_____	_____
_____	_____	_____	_____	_____
_____	_____	_____	_____	_____
	SUBTOTAL	$_____	$_____	$_____

6. Services

Include the cost of duplication and printing, long distance telephone, equipment rental, postage, and other services related to project objectives that are not included under other budget categories or in the indirect cost pool. For subcontracts over $10,000, provide an itemization of subcontract costs on this form or on an attachment.

item	basis/method of cost computation	(a)	(b)	(c)
_____	_____	$_____	$_____	$_____
_____	_____	_____	_____	_____
_____	_____	_____	_____	_____
_____	_____	_____	_____	_____
_____	_____	_____	_____	_____
_____	_____	_____	_____	_____
_____	_____	_____	_____	_____
	SUBTOTAL	$_____	$_____	$_____

Exhibit 36. NEH Grant Application Form (cont.).

7. Other Costs

Include participant stipends and room and board, equipment purchases, and other items not previously listed. Please note that "miscellaneous" and "contingency" are not acceptable budget categories. Refer to the budget instructions for the restriction on the purchase of permanent equipment.

item	basis/method of cost computation	NEH Funds (a)	Cost Sharing (b)	Total (c)
_____	_____	$_____	$_____	$_____
_____	_____	_____	_____	_____
_____	_____	_____	_____	_____
_____	_____	_____	_____	_____
_____	_____	_____	_____	_____
_____	_____	_____	_____	_____
_____	_____	_____	_____	_____
_____	_____	_____	_____	_____
	SUBTOTAL	$_____	$_____	$_____

8. Total Direct Costs (add subtotals of items 1 through 7)

$_____ $_____ $_____

9. Indirect Costs [This budget item applies only to institutional applicants.]

If indirect costs are to be charged to this project, check the appropriate box below and provide the information requested. Refer to the budget instructions for explanations of these options.

☐ Current indirect cost rate(s) has/have been negotiated with a federal agency. (Complete items A and B.)

☐ Indirect cost proposal has been submitted to a federal agency but not yet negotiated. (Indicate the name of the agency in item A and show proposed rate(s) and base(s), and the amount(s) of indirect costs in item B.)

☐ Indirect cost proposal will be sent to NEH if application is funded. (Provide an estimate in item B of the rate that will be used and indicate the base against which it will be charged and the amount of indirect costs.)

☐ Applicant chooses to use a rate not to exceed 10% of direct costs, less distorting items, up to a maximum charge of $5,000. (Under item B, enter the proposed rate, the base against which the rate will be charged, and the computation of indirect costs or $5,000, whichever sum is less.)

A. _____   _____
   name of federal agency   date of agreement

B.		NEH Funds (a)	Cost Sharing (b)	Total (c)
rate(s)	base(s)			
_____ %	of $_____	$_____	$_____	$_____
_____ %	of $_____	_____	_____	_____
	TOTAL INDIRECT COSTS	$_____	$_____	$_____

10. Total Project Costs (direct and indirect) for Budget Period

$_____ $_____ $_____

Exhibit 36. NEH Grant Application Form (cont.).

SECTION B — Summary Budget and Project Funding

SUMMARY BUDGET

Transfer from section A the total costs (column c) for each category of project expense. When the proposed grant period is eighteen months or longer, project expenses for each twelve-month period are to be listed separately and totaled in the last column of the summary budget. For projects that will run less than eighteen months, only the last column of the summary budget should be completed.

Budget Categories	First Year/ from: to:	Second Year/ from: to:	Third Year/ from: to:		TOTAL COSTS FOR ENTIRE GRANT PERIOD
1. Salaries and Wages	$_____	$_____	$_____	=	$_____
2. Fringe Benefits	_____	_____	_____	=	_____
3. Consultant Fees	_____	_____	_____	=	_____
4. Travel	_____	_____	_____	=	_____
5. Supplies and Materials	_____	_____	_____	=	_____
6. Services	_____	_____	_____	=	_____
7. Other Costs	_____	_____	_____	=	_____
8. **Total Direct Costs (items 1-7)**	$_____	$_____	$_____	=	$_____
9. Indirect Costs	$_____	$_____	$_____	=	$_____
10. **Total Project Costs (Direct & Indirect)**	$_____	$_____	$_____	=	$_____

PROJECT FUNDING FOR ENTIRE GRANT PERIOD

Requested from NEH:[1]

Outright $_____

Federal Matching $_____

TOTAL NEH FUNDING $_____

Cost Sharing:[2]

Cash Contributions $_____

In-Kind Contributions $_____

Project Income $_____

TOTAL COST SHARING $_____

Total Project Funding (NEH Funds + Cost Sharing)[3] = $_____

[1] Indicate the amount of outright and/or federal matching funds that is requested from the Endowment.

[2] Indicate the amount of cash contributions that will be made by the applicant or third parties to support project expenses that appear in the budget. Include in this amount third-party cash gifts that will be raised to release federal matching funds. (Consult the program guidelines for information on cost-sharing requirements.)

Occasionally, in-kind (noncash) contributions are included in a project budget as a part of the applicant's cost sharing; e.g., the value of services or equipment that is donated to the project free of charge. If this is the case, the total value of in-kind contributions should be indicated.

When a project will generate income that will be used during the grant period to support expenses listed in the budget, indicate the amount of income that will be expended on budgeted project activities.

[3] Total Project Funding should equal Total Project Costs.

Institutional Grant Administrator

Complete the information requested below when a revised budget is submitted. Block 11 of the application cover sheet instructions contains a description of the functions of the institutional grant administrator. The signature of this person indicates approval of the budget submission and the agreement of the organization to cost share project expenses at the level indicated under "Project Funding."

_____   Telephone ( )
Name and Title (please type or print)   area code

_____   Date _____
Signature

NEH Application/Grant Number: _____

G. NATIONAL SCIENCE FOUNDATION (NSF)

General

NSF uses the same proposal cover sheet for all programs. It is probably the simplest of all federal agency application forms (no OMB#) and should be no problem to complete.

Institutional Information Required

There is none beyond normal address and mailing information.

Project Questions

There are none except you are to check a box if the proposal involves any of the following: Animal Welfare, Endangered Species, Human Subjects, Historical Sites, Marine Mammal Protection, Pollution Control, National Environmental Policy Act, Recombinant DNA, and Proprietary and Privileged Information.

Exhibit 37. NSF Grant Application Form.

COVER SHEET FOR PROPOSALS TO THE
NATIONAL SCIENCE FOUNDATION

FOR CONSIDERATION BY NSF ORGANIZATIONAL UNIT (Indicate the most specific unit known, i.e. program, division, etc..)	PROGRAM ANNOUNCEMENT/SOLICITATION NO./CLOSING DATE **NSF 90-18**

SUBMITTING INSTITUTION CODE (If known)	FOR RENEWAL ☐ CONTINUING AWARD ☐ ACCOMPLISHMENT BASED RENEWAL ☐ REQUEST, LIST PREVIOUS AWARD NO.:	IS THIS PROPOSAL BEING SUBMITTED TO ANOTHER FEDERAL AGENCY? Yes____ No____; IF YES, LIST ACRONYM(S)

NAME OF SUBMITTING ORGANIZATION TO WHICH AWARD SHOULD BE MADE (INCLUDE BRANCH/CAMPUS/OTHER COMPONENTS)

ADDRESS OF ORGANIZATION (INCLUDE ZIP CODE)

IS SUBMITTING ORGANIZATION: ☐ For-Profit Organization; ☐ Small Business; ☐ Minority Business; ☐ Woman-Owned Business

TITLE OF PROPOSED PROJECT

REQUESTED AMOUNT	PROPOSED DURATION	DESIRED STARTING DATE

CHECK APPROPRIATE BOX(ES) IF THIS PROPOSAL INCLUDES ANY OF THE ITEMS LISTED BELOW:

☐ Animal Welfare	☐ National Environmental Policy Act	☐ International Cooperative Activity
☐ Endangered Species	☐ Research Involving Recombinant DNA Molecules	☐ Research Opportunity Award
☐ Human Subjects		☐ Facilitation Award for Handicapped
☐ Marine Mammal Protection	☐ Historical Sites	☐ Proprietary and Privileged Information
☐ Pollution Control	☐ Interdisciplinary	

PI/PD DEPARTMENT	PI/PD ORGANIZATION	PI/PD PHONE NO. & ELECTRONIC MAIL

PI/PD NAME/TITLE	SOCIAL SECURITY NO.*	HIGHEST DEGREE & YEAR	SIGNATURE
ADDITIONAL PI/PD (TYPED)			
ADDITIONAL PI/PD (TYPED)			
ADDITIONAL PI/PD (TYPED)			
ADDITIONAL PI/PD (TYPED)			

For NSF Use:

TO BE COMPLETED BY THE AUTHORIZED ORGANIZATIONAL REPRESENTATIVE. By signing and submitting this proposal, the prospective grantee is providing the certifications set forth in (1) *Grants for Research and Education in Science and Engineering*, NSF 83-57 (rev. 11/87), and (2) Appendix C, 45CFR 620, Subpart F (Requirements for a Drug-Free Workplace).

(If answering *yes* to either, please provide explanation.)	YES	NO
Is the organization delinquent on any Federal Debt?		
Is the organization presently debarred, suspended, proposed for debarment, declared ineligible, or voluntarily excluded from covered transactions by any Federal department or agency?		

AUTHORIZED ORGANIZATIONAL REP.	SIGNATURE	DATE	TELEPHONE NO.
NAME/TITLE (TYPED)			

OTHER ENDORSEMENT (optional)			
NAME/TITLE (TYPED)			

*Submission of social security numbers is voluntary and will not affect the organization's eligibility for an award. However, they are an integral part of the NSF information system and assist in processing the proposal. SSN solicited under NSF Act of 1950, as amended.

NSF Form 1207 (3/89)

Exhibit 37. NSF Grant Application Form (cont.).

INSTRUCTIONS FOR USE OF SUMMARY PROPOSAL BUDGET
(NSF FORM 1030)

1. General

a. Each grant proposal, including requests for supplemental funding, must contain a Summary Proposal Budget in this format unless a pertinent program guideline specifically provides otherwise. A Summary Proposal Budget need not be submitted for incremental funding unless the original grant letter did not indicate specific incremental funding or if adjustments to the planned increment exceeding 10% or $10,000 are being requested.

b. Copies of NSF Form 1030 and instructions should be reproduced locally as NSF will not supply the form.

c. A separate form should be completed for each year of support requested. An additional form showing the cuculative budget for the full term requested should be completed for proposals requesting more than one year's support. Identify each year's request (e.g., "First year _____," or "Cumulative Budget," etc.) in the margin at the top right of the form.

d. Completion of this summary does not eliminate the need to fully document and justify the amounts requested in each category. Such documentation should be provided on additional page(s) immediately following the budget in the proposal and should be identified by line item. The documentation page(s) should be titled "Budget Explanation Page."

e. If a revised budget is required by NSF, it must be signed and dated by the Authorized Organizational Representative and Principal Investigator and submitted in at least the original and two copies.

2. Budget Line Items

A full discussion of the budget and the allowability of selected items of cost is contained in Grants for Research and Education in Science and Engineering, NSF Grant Policy Manual—GPM (NSF 88-47 periodically revised), and other NSF program brochures and guidelines. Following is a brief outline of budget documentation requirements by line item. (NOTE: All documentation or justification required on the line items below should be provided on the Budget Explanation Page.)

A., B., and C. Salaries, Wages, and Fringe Benefits (GPM 511 and GPM 205.1). On the Budget Explanation Page, list individually all senior personnel who were grouped under A5, the requested person-months to be funded, and rates of pay.

D. Permanent Equipment (GPM 512 and 204.2). While items exceeding $500 and 2 years' useful life are defined as permanent equipment, it is only necessary to list item and dollar amount for each item exceeding $1,000. Fully justify.

E. Travel (GPM 514 and GPM 730). Address the type and extent of travel (including consultant travel) and its relation to the project. Itemize by destination and cost and justify travel outside the United States and its possessions, Puerto Rico, and Canada. Include dates of foreign visits or meetings. Fare allowances are limited to round-trip, jet-economy rates.

F. Participant Support Costs (GPM 518). Normally participant support may only be requested for grants supporting conferences, workshops or symposia. Show number of participants in brackets. Consult Grants for Research and Education in Science and Engineering or specific program guidelines.

G. Other Direct Costs.

1. Materials and Supplies (GPM 513). Indicate types required and estimate costs.

2. Publication, Documentation, Dissemination (GPM 517). Estimate costs of documenting, preparing, publishing, disseminating, and sharing research findings.

3. Consultant Services (GPM 516). Indicate name, daily compensation (limited to GS-18 daily rate), and estimated days of service, and justify.

4. Computer Services (GPM 515). Include justification based on established computer service rates at the proposing institution. Purchase of equipment is included under D.

5. Subcontracts (GPM 623 and Exh. V-1). Include a complete budget and justify details.

6. Other. Itemize and justify. Include computer equipment leasing.

I. Indirect Costs (GPM 530). Specify current rate(s) and base(s). Use current rate(s) negotiated with the cognizant Federal negotiating agency. See GPM for special policy regarding grants to individuals, travel grants, equipment grants, doctoral dissertation grants, and grants involving participant support costs (chap. V, GPM).

K. Residual Funds (GPM 253). For incremental funding requests on continuing grants, enter the amount estimated to be in excess of 20% at the planned amendment effective date. If less than 20%, indicate: "none." Residual funds should not be reflected in budget categories A-I. A justification for carryover of funds in excess of 20% is required.

L. Item L will be the same as Item J unless the Foundation disapproves the carryover of funds. If disapproved, Item L will equal J minus K.

APPLICANTS MUST NOT ALTER OR REARRANGE THE COST CATEGORIES AS THEY APPEAR ON THIS FORM. WHICH IS DESIGNED FOR COMPATIBILITY WITH DATA CAPTURE BY NSF'S MANAGEMENT INFORMATION SYSTEM. IMPROPER COMPLETION OF THIS FORM MAY RESULT IN RETURN OF PROPOSAL TO APPLICANT.

30

Exhibit 37. NSF Grant Application Form (cont.).

(SEE INSTRUCTIONS ON REVERSE BEFORE COMPLETING	**SUMMARY PROPOSAL BUDGET**	FOR NSF USE ONLY		
ORGANIZATION		PROPOSAL NO.	DURATION (MONTHS)	
			Proposed	Granted
PRINCIPAL INVESTIGATOR/PROJECT DIRECTOR		AWARD NO.		

A. SENIOR PERSONNEL: PI/PD. Co-PI's, Faculty and Other Senior Associates (List each separately with title, A.6. show number in brackets)	NSF Funded Person-mos.			Funds Requested By Proposer	Funds Granted By NSF (If Different)
	CAL.	ACAD	SUMR		
1.				$	$
2.					
3.					
4.					
5. ( ) OTHERS (LIST INDIVIDUALLY ON BUDGET EXPLANATION PAGE)					
6. ( ) TOTAL SENIOR PERSONNEL (1-5)					
B. OTHER PERSONNEL (SHOW NUMBERS IN BRACKETS)					
1. ( ) POST DOCTORAL ASSOCIATES					
2. ( ) OTHER PROFESSIONALS (TECHNICIAN, PROGRAMMER, ETC.)					
3. ( ) GRADUATE STUDENTS					
4. ( ) UNDERGRADUATE STUDENTS					
5. ( ) SECRETARIAL CLERICAL					
6. ( ) OTHER					
TOTAL SALARIES AND WAGES (A+B)					
C. FRINGE BENEFITS (IF CHARGED AS DIRECT COSTS)					
TOTAL SALARAIES, WAGES AND FRINGE BENEFITS (A+B+C)					
D. PERMANENT EQUIPMENT (LIST ITEM AND DOLLAR AMOUNT FOR EACH ITEM EXCEEDING $1,000:)					
TOTAL PERMANENT EQUIPMENT					
E. TRAVEL 1. DOMESTIC (INCL. CANADA AND U.S. POSSESSIONS)					
2. FOREIGN					
F. PARTICIPANT SUPPORT COSTS					
1. STIPENDS $ _____					
2. TRAVEL _____					
3. SUBSISTENCE _____					
4. OTHER _____					
( ) TOTAL PARTICIPANT COSTS					
G. OTHER DIRECT COSTS					
1. MATERIALS AND SUPPLIES					
2. PUBLICATION COSTS/DOCUMENTATION/DISSEMINATION					
3. CONSULTANT SERVICES					
4. COMPUTER (ADPE) SERVICES					
5. SUBCONTRACTS					
6. OTHER					
TOTAL OTHER DIRECT COSTS					
H. TOTAL DIRECT COSTS (A THROUGH G)					
I. INDIRECT COSTS (SPECIFY RATE AND BASE)					
TOTAL INDIRECT COSTS					
J. TOTAL DIRECT AND INDIRECT COSTS (H + I)					
K. RESIDUAL FUNDS (IF FOR FURTHER SUPPORT OF CURRENT PROJECTS SEE GPM 252 AND 253)					
L. AMOUNT OF THIS REQUEST (J) OR (J MINUS K)				$	$

PI/PD TYPED NAME & SIGNATURE*	DATE	FOR NSF USE ONLY		
		INDIRECT COST RATE VERIFICATION		
INST. REP. TYPED NAME & SIGNATURE*	DATE	Date Checked	Date of Rate Sheet	Inititals-DGC

NSF Form 1030 (8/90) *Supersedes All Previous Editions*   *SIGNATURES REQUIRED ONLY FOR REVISED BUDGET (GPM 233)

29

H. U.S. DEPARTMENT OF AGRICULTURE (USDA)

General

The USDA requires the submission of OMB form # 0524-00022 for competitive, special, or other research grants from the Cooperative State Research Service. The application kit can also be used for other funds awarded by CSRS.

Institutional Information Required

Along with standard applicant and project information, there are several items of information needed to complete the application forms that may not be readily accessible. Therefore, you should have them in advance to make completion of the form easier. These are:

1. Congressional district;
2. Program to which you are applying (as listed in the *Federal Register* announcement);
3. Federal Employment Identification No. (IRS#);
4. Type of performing organization the applicant is (list provided—select one).

Project Questions

There are two questions relating to submission that must be answered by submitting institution. They are:

1. Does the project involve recombinant DNA or human subjects?
2. Was the proposal sent to another federal agency and which one?

Other required and useful information with suggested forms: example of a budget, letter of transmittal, and protection of human subject certification.

Exhibit 38. USDA Grant Application Form.

<table>
<tr><td colspan="2" style="text-align:center">FOR CSRS USE ONLY</td><td colspan="2" style="text-align:center">UNITED STATES DEPARTMENT OF AGRICULTURE
COOPERATIVE STATE RESEARCH SERVICE

GRANT APPLICATION</td><td>OMB Approved 0524-0022
Expires 8/92</td></tr>
<tr><td>Program Area Code</td><td>Proposal Code</td></tr>
</table>

1. Legal Name of Organization to Which Award Should be Made	3. Name of Authorized Organizational Representative	4. Telephone Number (Include Area Code)
2. Address (Give complete mailing address and Zip Code-including County)	5. Address of Authorized Organizational Representative (If different from Item 2.)	

6. Title of Proposal (80-character Maximum, including spaces)

7. Program to Which You are Applying (Refer to Federal Register Announcement where applicable)	8. Program Area and Number (Refer to Federal Register Announcement where applicable)

9. IRS No.	10. Congressional District No.	11. Period of Proposed Project Dates From: Through:	12. Duration Requested

13. Type of Request

☐ New   ☐ Resubmission   ☐ Renewal   ☐ Supplement   ☐ Continuing Grant Increment

☐ PI Transfer   ☐ (of/to USDA Grant No. _____)   ☐ Other

14. Funds Requested (From Form CSRS-55)

15. Principal Investigator(s)/Project Director(s) a. PI/PD #1 Name (First, Middle, Last) and Social Security Number* (Correspondent PI)	**16. PI/PD #1 Phone Number** (Include Area Code)
b. PI/PD #2 Name (First, Middle, Last) and Social Security Number*	**17. PI/PD #1 Business Address** (Include Department/Zip Code)
c. PI/PD #3 Name (First, Middle, Last) and Social Security Number*	

Submission of the Social Security Number is voluntary and will not affect the organization's eligibility for an award. However, it is an integral part of the CSRS information system and will assist in the processing of the proposal.

18. Type of Performing Organization
(Check one only)

01 ☐ USDA/S&E Laboratory
02 ☐ Other Federal Research Laboratory
03 ☐ State Agricultural Experiment Station (SAES)
04 ☐ Land-Grant University 1862
05 ☐ Land-Grant University 1890 or Tuskegee University
06 ☐ Private University or College
07 ☐ Public University or College (Non Land-Grant)
08 ☐ Private Profit-making
09 ☐ Private Non-profit
10 ☐ State or Local Government
11 ☐ Veterinary School or College
12 ☐ Other (Specify)

19. Will the Work in This Proposal Involve Recombinant DNA?

☐ No   ☐ Yes (If yes, complete Form CSRS-662)

20. Will the Work in This Proposal Involve Living Vertebrate Animals?

☐ No   ☐ Yes (If yes, complete Form CSRS-662)

21. Will the Work in This Proposal Involve Human Subjects?

☐ No   ☐ Yes (If yes, complete Form CSRS-662)

22. Will This Proposal be Sent or has it Been Sent to Other Funding Agencies, Including Other USDA Agencies?

☐ No   ☐ Yes (If yes, list Agency acronym(s) & program(s))

By signing and submitting this proposal, the prospective grantee is providing the required certifications set forth in 7 CFR Part 3017, as amended, regarding Debarment and Suspension and Drug-Free Workplace; and 7 CFR Part 3018 regarding Lobbying. **Submission of the individual forms is not required.** (Please read the Certifications and Instructions included in this kit before signing this form.)

In addition, the prospective grantee certifies that the information contained herein is true and complete to the best of its knowledge and accepts as to any grant award, the obligation to comply with the terms and conditions of Cooperative State Research Service in effect at the time of the award.

Signature of Principal Investigator(s)/Project Director(s) (All PI's/PD's listed in block 15 must sign if they are to be included in award document.)	Date

Signature of Authorized Organizational Representative (Same as Item 3)	Title	Date

Form CSRS-661 (9/89)

Exhibit 38. USDA Grant Application Form (cont.).

UNITED STATES DEPARTMENT OF AGRICULTURE
COOPERATIVE STATE RESEARCH SERVICE

BUDGET

OMB Approved 0524-0022
Expires 8/92

Organization and Address	USDA Grant No.	
	Duration Proposed Months: _____ **FUNDS REQUESTED BY PROPOSER**	Duration Awarded Months: _____ **FUNDS APPROVED BY CSRS** (If different)

Principal Investigator(s)/Project Director(s) _____

		CSRS FUNDED WORK MONTHS			FUNDS REQUESTED BY PROPOSER	FUNDS APPROVED BY CSRS
		Calendar	Academic	Summer		
A.	Salaries and Wages					
	1. No. of Senior Personnel					
	a. _____ (Co)-PI(s)/PD(s).				$	$
	b. _____ Senior Associates					
	2. No. of Other Personnel (Non-Faculty)					
	a. _____ Research Associates-Postdoctorate					
	b. _____ Other Professionals					
	c. _____ Graduate Students					
	d. _____ Prebaccalaureate Students					
	e. _____ Secretarial-Clerical					
	f. _____ Technical, Shop and Other					
	Total Salaries and Wages . . . . ➤					
B.	Fringe Benefits (If charged as Direct Costs)					
C.	**Total Salaries, Wages, and Fringe Benefits** (A plus B) . . . . ➤					
D.	Nonexpendable Equipment (Attach supporting data. List items and dollar amounts for **each** item.)					
E.	Materials and Supplies					
F.	Travel					
	1. Domestic (Including Canada)					
	2. Foreign (List destination and amount for each trip.)					
G.	Publication Costs/Page Charges					
H.	Computer (ADPE) Costs					
I.	All Other Direct Costs (Attach supporting data. List items and dollar amounts. Details of subcontracts, including work statements and budget, should be explained in full in proposal.)					
J.	**Total Direct Costs** (C through I) . . . . ➤					
K.	**Indirect Costs** (Specify rate(s) and base(s) for on/off campus activity. Where both are involved, identify itemized costs included in on/off campus bases.)					
L.	**Total Direct and Indirect Costs** (J plus K) . . . . ➤					
M.	**Other** . . . . ➤					
N.	**Total Amount of This Request** . . . . ➤				$	$
O.	**Cost Sharing**	$				

NOTE: Signatures required only for Revised Budget   *This is Revision No.* ➤

Name and Title (Type or print)	Signature	Date
Principal Investigator/Project Director		
Authorized Organizational Representative		

Form CSRS-55 (9/89)

I. OTHER REQUIRED FORMS AND NECESSARY INFORMATION

1. Examples of an Application Form and Guidelines from Two Private Foundations

Exhibit 39. Application Form from a Private Foundation.

Application Form

Mary Reynolds Babcock Foundation

102 Reynolda Village Winston-Salem, North Carolina 27106-5123
Telephone 919/748-9222
Telefax 919/777-0095

Please check off items on the list below and return the application with all items attached. If an item is omitted, your application may have to be deferred until the next deadline.

The Mary Reynolds Babcock Foundation provides grants to tax-exempt organizations for programs primarily in the following areas: environmental protection, development of public policy, education, government accountability, well-being of children and adolescents, philanthropy, the arts, grassroots organizing, rural issues, and women's concerns. The majority (75 percent) of grants are made to organizations working in North Carolina and the Southeast. Additional information about program interests is contained in the foundation's annual report, available upon request.

The foundation also provides program-related investments (loans) in the same areas of interest supported by grants. Qualified applicants are intermediary organizations, tax-exempt lending institutions which offer technical assistance in conjunction with their loans. Applicants for program-related investments should contact the foundation staff before submitting their application.

The board of directors meets in May and November to consider grant applications. All of the following materials should be post-marked by the application deadlines, March 1 and September 1, preceding each meeting. If these dates fall on a weekend or holiday, the first business day following the date becomes the deadline.

☐ **Application form.** This form with all four pages completed, including an authorized signature on the second page. *Give particular attention* to the proposal summary, which should be typed, on the last page.

☐ **Proposal.** A program description of *no more than five pages,* stating the following:

Need for the program
Objectives and purposes of the program
How the objectives and purposes of the program
  are to be met
Description of the applying organization
Qualifications of the staff
Location and estimated duration of the program
Planned method and criteria for evaluation of the program

☐ **Budgets.** Separate one-page, line-item budgets identifying the projected income and expenses of the organization and the program.

☐ **Board of directors.** A list of the members of the sponsoring organization's governing board with identification of their organizational affiliation or occupation.

☐ **Certificate of tax-exempt status.** A copy of the sponsoring organization's letter of tax exemption from the Internal Revenue Service. The letter should indicate whether the organization is a private foundation under the 1969 Tax Reform Act. Governmental agencies need not submit a tax-exempt letter. Contact the foundation staff if the organization has applied for, but not yet received, tax-exempt status.

☐ **Optional materials.** Additional descriptive materials may be submitted with the application. A news article or brochure describing the organization is appropriate.

In developing your proposal, please consider that the foundation ordinarily does not provide funds for projects within the following categories:

Brick-and-mortar projects
Assistance to individuals, such as scholarships or
  fellowships
International programs
Film and video production
Health and medical programs
Tax-supported educational institutions outside
  North Carolina
Research programs
Endowments

Exhibit 39. Application Form from a Private Foundation (cont.)

About the applicant . . .

All information on this page concerns the organization applying for the grant and responsible agent for any funds received.

Organization applying for grant

Name _____

Address _____

_____ telephone (_____) _____

Chief administrative officer _____ title _____

Fiscal information

Beginning and ending dates of your fiscal year _____ to _____

Total current assets (market value) of organization $ _____

Total current endowment (market value) $ _____

Total current fund balance $ _____

Date of incorporation _____

Total expenditures for last three years

| 19_____ | 19_____ | 19_____ |
| $_____ | $_____ | $_____ |

Date of organization's last outside and unqualified audit _____

Tax-exempt status

Have you attached a copy of your IRS determination letter(s)? _____ If your organization is awaiting a response from IRS,

please check this box ☐ and give date of application _____ Note: This does not apply to governmental agencies.

Signature

_____

Approval of board chairman or executive officer   Title   Date

If your organization is a private educational institution, the signature on this form certifies that your institution has complied with IRS Procedure 75-50 for adoption and publication of a racially nondiscriminatory policy.

Exhibit 39. Application Form from a Private Foundation (cont.).

About the program . . .

Information on this page concerns the program for which funding is requested.

General information

Program title _____

Beginning and ending dates of program _____ to _____

Dates for which funding is requested _____ to _____

Program director's name _____ title _____

Address _____

_____ telephone (_____) _____

Total program budget $ _____ Amount requested of MRBF $ _____

Potential funding

What funds from other private or public sources have been received or are under consideration for this program? Please list amounts requested from other sources (for example, XYZ Foundation—$10,000).

Received	Under Consideration

Future funding

If the program is to continue beyond the grant period, what are the plans for funding of the program upon expenditure of this grant?

Exhibit 39. Application Form from a Private Foundation (cont.).

Proposal summary

Name of applicant organization _____ City _____ State _____

Program Title _____

Total program budget $ _____ Amount requested from MRBF $ _____

Please summarize below the need for the program and how the program seeks to meet the need.

Exhibit 40. Application Guidelines from a Private Foundation.

Application Guidelines

Who Is Eligible

The Trusts make grants to organizations classified as tax exempt under section 501(c)(3) of the Internal Revenue Service Code and as public charities under sections 509(a)(1), (2), and (3) of the code.

Applying for a Grant

LETTER OF INQUIRY

Grant application at the Trusts is essentially a two-stage process. In the first stage, organizations should request and carefully review the Trusts' guidelines to determine if their project or organization qualifies for funding. If there appears to be a match, applicants should submit a brief letter of inquiry (no longer than five pages) summarizing the project for which they are requesting support. Because of the large number of requests we receive and the time entailed to develop a proposal, we urge applicants not to send in full proposals before they have had preliminary contact with the program staff and been encouraged to proceed. The Trusts will respond to all formal letters of inquiry but not to general solicitations for funds.

PROPOSAL

After letters of inquiry are reviewed by staff, applicants will be notified either by phone or letter if their request falls within the funding priorities and guidelines of the Trusts; if so, they may be asked at that time to develop a full proposal. An application package will then be sent outlining all the information that should be included in the proposal.

The second stage of the application process begins with receipt of the applicant's full proposal, which is evaluated by staff within the context of the Trusts' guidelines, funding priorities, and available resources. After initial staff evaluation, a certain number of proposals are forwarded to the Trusts' board for final review and approval. This second stage of the application process normally takes from three to six months. Historically, one in fifteen proposals submitted is approved for funding.

General Information

Grants are awarded five times a year, in February, April, June, September, and December. Most proposals are accepted year round; however, certain categories of requests are scheduled for review at specific board meetings. Any special submission deadlines are noted on the following pages of this brochure in the relevant program sections. Organizations whose proposals are turned down for funding must wait a minimum of twelve months before submitting another request for consideration (This does not apply to letters of inquiry).

New requests from previously funded organizations will be reviewed only after the grant period for any previous award from the Trusts has expired and all reporting conditions, including those in any grant modifications, have been met.

Occasionally, the Trusts will invite organizations to develop a specific proposal or participate in a trust-initiated program. Proposals submitted at the invitation of the Trusts or participation in a trust-initiated program will have no effect on an organization's ability to submit its own independent request.

Organizations are encouraged to seek funding for proposed projects from multiple sources. The Trusts' approval of a grant should not be taken as an implied commitment to continued or future support.

Please address letters of inquiry to The Pew Charitable Trusts, Three Parkway, Suite 501, Philadelphia, PA 19102-1305. One person, preferably the chief executive officer, principal investigator, or other authorized representative, should be identified as the primary contact.

Organizations with questions about eligibility or deadlines are encouraged to call the program offices listed on pages 23 and 24 or the Communications office at (215) 587-4056.

2. A Format for a *Curriculum Vitae*

Use of a standardized and easy-to-follow form helps the reviewer. Your *curriculum vitae* should provide a good profile of your background and current activities. If you are applying for support for some project not directly related to your professional experience, or if you are presenting a research project, you should add a statement giving information demonstrating your competency in the activities described in the proposal.

Exhibit 41. *Curriculum Vitae.*

```
This is a recommended format for curriculum vitae.  Provide the
information in the order suggested following headlines and in-
structions.  Space headings as required by the answers.

                       CURRICULUM VITAE
NAME:  (first, middle, last) (repeat name on each sheet)

ADDRESS:                        PHONE:  (off.) (---)---/----
                                        (home) (---)---/----

PRESENT POSITION:  (title, rank, department as appropriate)

EDUCATION:  Degree    Institution    Location    Date    Major
            (undergraduate first) (state/branch) (of degree)
            (A.B.)    _____     _____      ____    ____
            (M.A.)    _____     _____      ____    ____
            (Ph.D.)   _____     _____      ____    ____

PROFESSIONAL EXPERIENCE:

   19__ to present  (repeat present position)

   19__ to 19__     (start with latest position and work backwards)

                    (include all paid positions, full-time and part-
                    time in your present field of work and all other
                    work experience including military service)


AWARDS, GRANTS & SPECIAL PROJECTS:  (fellowships, traineeships,
                                    research not included under
                                    publication section.  Add a
                                    heading for research if you
                                    prefer)


MEMBERSHIPS & VOLUNTEER ACTIVITIES  (list most important to you for
                                    any date and those which are
                                    current)


PUBLICATIONS:  (start with current publications and work backwards.
               Some agencies ask that you limit publications to
               those completed in the last three to ten years.
               Continue on additional pages if needed.)


        Name of institution: (repeat on each sheet
        Date:  (date when this information was prepared)
```

3. Acknowledgment Card

Most agencies use such cards that you address to yourself, your Chief Administrative Officer, and your Grants Officer. The returned receipt will have a document number to identify your proposal. *Don't lose it.* It is the only way your proposal can be found if you have questions. It is also proof that your proposal was received in time.

Exhibit 42. Acknowledgment Card.

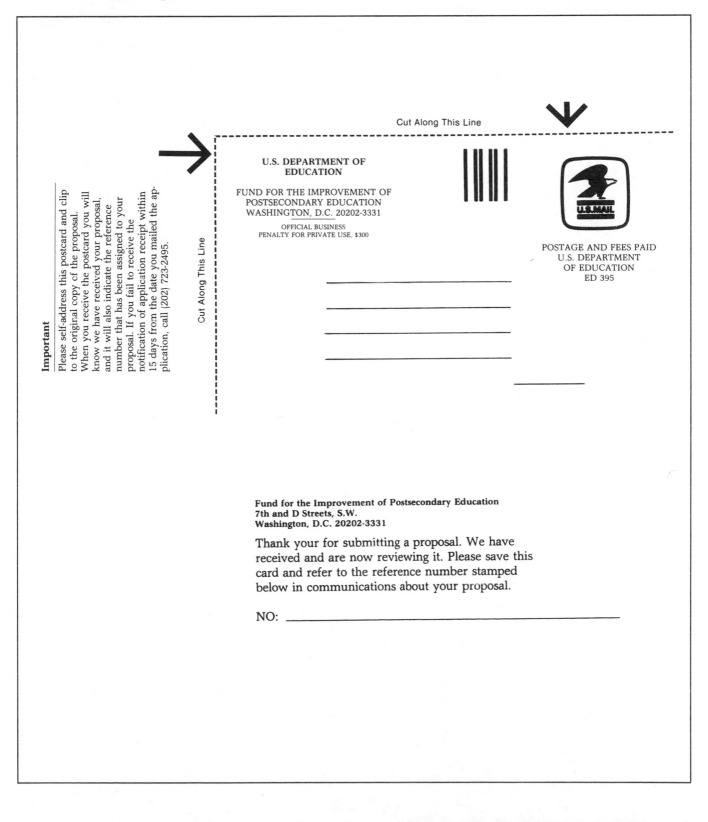

Important

Please self-address this postcard and clip to the original copy of the proposal. When you receive the postcard you will know we have received your proposal, and it will also indicate the reference number that has been assigned to your proposal. If you fail to receive the notification of application receipt within 15 days from the date you mailed the application, call (202) 723-2495.

Cut Along This Line

Cut Along This Line

U.S. DEPARTMENT OF EDUCATION

FUND FOR THE IMPROVEMENT OF POSTSECONDARY EDUCATION WASHINGTON, D.C. 20202-3331

OFFICIAL BUSINESS
PENALTY FOR PRIVATE USE, $300

POSTAGE AND FEES PAID
U.S. DEPARTMENT
OF EDUCATION
ED 395

Fund for the Improvement of Postsecondary Education
7th and D Streets, S.W.
Washington, D.C. 20202-3331

Thank your for submitting a proposal. We have received and are now reviewing it. Please save this card and refer to the reference number stamped below in communications about your proposal.

NO: _____

4. Certification and Assurance Forms and Regulations

The information and forms included here cover most of the federal compliance requirements. The first, Exhibit 43, is a list of most of the required assurances. This is followed by Exhibit 44, the Civil Rights Certificate; Exhibit 45, Protection of Human Subjects Assurance; Exhibit 46, Certifications Regarding Lobbying, Debarment, Suspension, and Other Responsibility Matters (and a similar form from the USDA, Exhibit 47); and Drug Free Workplace Requirements; form for Disclosure of Lobbying Activities, Exhibit 48; and finally the Certification Regarding Drug-Free Workplace Requirements for Grantees Other than Individuals.

Exhibit 43. List of Required Assurances.

Assurances

The Applicant hereby assures and certifies that it will comply with the regulations, policies, guidelines and requirements, as they relate to the application, acceptance and use of Federal funds for this federally-assisted project. Also the Applicant assures and certifies:

1. It possesses legal authority to apply for the grant; that a resolution, motion or similar action has been duly adopted or passed as an official act of the applicant's governing body, authorizing the filing of the application, including all understandings and assurances contained therein, and directing and authorizing the person identified as the official representative of the applicant to act in connection with the application and to provide such additional information as may be required.

2. It will comply with Title VI of the Civil Rights Act of 1964 (P.L. 88-352) and in accordance with Title VI of the Act, no person in the United States shall, on the grounds of race, color or national origin, be excluded from participation in, be denied the benefits of, or be otherwise subjected to discrimination under any program or activity for which the applicant receives Federal financial assistance and will immediately take any measures necessary to effectuate this agreement.

3. It will comply with Title VI of the Civil Rights Act of 1964 (42 U.S.C. 2000d) prohibiting employment discrimination where (1) the primary purpose of a grant is to provide employment or (2) discriminatory employment practices will result in unequal treatment of persons who are or should be benefiting from the grant-aided activity.

4. It will comply with Section 504 of the Rehabilitation Act of 1973, as amended, 29 U.S.C. 794, which prohibits discrimination on the basis of handicap in programs and activities receiving Federal financial assistance.

5. It will comply with Title IX of the Education Amendments of 1972, as amended, 20 U.S.C. 1681 et seq., which prohibits discrimination on the basis of sex in education programs and activities receiving Federal financial assistance.

6. It will comply with the Age Discrimination Act of 1975, as amended, 42 U.S.C. 6101 et seq., which prohibits discrimination on the basis of age in programs or activities receiving Federal financial assistance.

7. It will comply with requirements of the provisions of the Uniform Relocation Assistance and Real Property Acquisitions Act of 1970 (P.L. 91-646) which provides for fair and equitable treatment of persons displaced as a result of Federal and Federally-assisted programs.

8. It will comply with the provisions of the Hatch Act which limit the political activity of employees.

9. It will comply with the minimum wage and maximum hours provisions of the Federal Fair Labor Standards Act, as they apply to hospital and educational institution employees of State and local governments.

10. It will establish safeguards to prohibit employees from using their positions for a purpose that is or gives the appearance of being motivated by a desire for private gain for themselves or others, particularly those with whom they have family, business, or other ties.

11. It will give the sponsoring agency or the Comptroller General through any authorized representative the access to and the right to examine all records, books, papers, or documents related to the grant.

12. It will comply with all requirements imposed by the Federal sponsoring agency concerning special requirements of law, program requirements, and other administrative requirements.

13. It will insure that the facilities under its ownership, lease or supervision which shall be utilized in the accomplishment of the project are not listed on the Environmental Protection Agency's (EPA) list of Violating Facilities and that it will notify the Federal grantor agency of the receipt of any communication from the Director of the EPA Office of Federal Activities indicating that a facility to be used in the project is under consideration for listing by the EPA.

14. It will comply with the flood insurance purchase requirements of Section 102(a) of the Flood Disaster Protection Act of 1973, P.L. 93-234, 87 Stat. 975, approved December 31, 1976. Section 102(a) requires, on or after March 2, 1975, the purchase of flood insurance in communities where such insurance is available as a condition for the receipt of any Federal financial assistance for construction or acquisition purposes for use in any area that has been identified by the Secretary of the Department of Housing and Urban Development as an area having special flood hazards. The phrase "Federal financial assistance" includes any form of loan, grant, guaranty, insurance payment, rebate, subsidy, disaster assistance loan or grant, or any other form of direct or indirect Federal assistance.

15. It will assist the Federal grantor agency in its compliance with Section 106 of the National Historic Preservation Act of 1966 as amended (16 U.S.C. 470), Executive Order 11593, and the Archeological and Historic Preservation Act of 1966 (16 U.S.C. 469a-1 et seq.) by (a) consulting with the State Historic Preservation Officer on the conduct of investigations, as necessary, to identify properties listed in or eligible for inclusion in the National Register of Historic Places that are subject to adverse effects (see 36 CFR Part 800.8) by the activity, and notifying the Federal grantor agency of the existence of any such properties, and by (b) complying with all requirements established by the Federal grantor agency to avoid or mitigate adverse effects upon such properties.

Exhibit 44. Civil Rights Certificate.

CIVIL RIGHTS CERTIFICATE

ASSURANCE OF COMPLIANCE WITH TITLE VI OF THE CIVIL RIGHTS ACT OF 1964, SECTION 504 OF THE REHABILITATION ACT OF 1973, TITLE IX OF THE EDUCATION AMENDMENTS OF 1972, AND THE AGE DISCRIMINATION ACT OF 1975

The applicant provides this assurance in consideration of and for the purpose of obtaining Federal grants, loans, contracts (except contracts of insurance or guaranty), property, discounts, or other Federal financial assistance to education programs or activities from the Department of Education.

The applicant assures that it will comply with:

1. Title VI of the Civil Rights Act of 1964, as amended, 42 U.S.C. 2000d *et seq.,* which prohibits discrimination on the basis of race, color, or national origin in programs and activities receiving Federal financial assistance.

2. Section 504 of the Rehabilitation Act of 1973, as amended, 29 U.S.C. 794, which prohibits discrimination on the basis of handicap in programs and activities receiving Federal financial assistance.

3. Title IX of the Education Amendments of 1972, as amended, 20 U.S.C. 1681 *et seq.,* which prohibits discrimination on the basis of sex in education programs and activities receiving Federal financial assistance.

4. The Age Discrimination Act of 1975, as amended, 42 U.S.C. 6101 *et seq.,* which prohibits discrimination on the basis of age in programs or activities receiving Federal financial assistance.

5. All regulations, guidelines, and standards lawfully adopted under the above statutes by the United States Department of Education.

The applicant agrees that compliance with this Assurance constitutes a condition of continued receipt of Federal finan assistance, and that it is binding upon the applicant, its successors, transferees, and assignees for the period during which such assistance is provided. The applicant further assures that all contractors, subcontractors, subgrantees or others with whom it arranges to provide services or benefits to its students or employees in connection with its education programs or activities are not discriminating in violation of the above statutes, regulations, guidelines, and standards against those students or employees. In the event of failure to comply the applicant understands that assistance can be terminated and the applicant denied the right to receive further assistance. The applicant also understands that the Department of Education may at its discretion seek a court order requiring compliance with the terms of the Assurance or seek other appropriate judicial relief.

The person or persons whose signature(s) appear(s) below is/are authorized to sign this application, and to commit the applicant to the above provisions.

_____
Date

_____
Authorized Official(s)

_____
Name of Applicant or Recipient

_____
Street

_____
City, State, Zip Code

Exhibit 45. Protection of Human Subjects Assurance.

OMB No. 0925-0637

DEPARTMENT OF HEALTH AND HUMAN SERVICES

PROTECTION OF HUMAN SUBJECTS ASSURANCE/CERTIFICATION/DECLARATION

☐ GRANT   ☐ CONTRACT   ☐ FELLOW   ☐ OTHER

☐ New   ☐ Competing continuation   ☐ Noncompeting continuation   ☐ Supplemental

☐ ORIGINAL   ☐ FOLLOWUP   ☐ EXEMPTION (previously undesignated)

APPLICATION IDENTIFICATION NO. *(if known)*

POLICY: *A research activity involving human subjects that is not exempt from HHS regulations may not be funded unless an Institutional Review Board (IRB) has reviewed and approved the activity in accordance with Section 474 of the Public Health Service Act as implemented by Title 45, Part 46 of the Code of Federal Regulations (45 CFR 46—as revised). The applicant institution must submit certification of IRB approval to HHS unless the applicant institution has designated a specific exemption under Section 46.101(b) which applies to the proposed research activity. Institutions with an assurance of compliance on file with HHS which covers the proposed activity should submit certification of IRB review and approval with each application. (In exceptional cases, certification may be accepted up to 60 days after the receipt date for which the application is submitted.) In the case of institutions which do not have an assurance of compliance on file with HHS covering the proposed activity, certification of IRB review and approval must be submitted within 30 days of the receipt of a written request from HHS for certification.*

1. TITLE OF APPLICATION OR ACTIVITY

2. PRINCIPAL INVESTIGATOR, PROGRAM DIRECTOR, OR FELLOW

3. FOOD AND DRUG ADMINISTRATION REQUIRED INFORMATION *(see reverse side)*

4. HHS ASSURANCE STATUS

☐ This institution has an approved assurance of compliance on file with HHS which covers this activity.

_____ Assurance identification number   _____ IRB identification number

☐ No assurance of compliance which applies to this activity has been established with HHS but the applicant institution will provide written assurance of compliance and certification of IRB review and approval in accordance with 45 CFR 46 upon request.

5. CERTIFICATION OF IRB REVIEW OR DECLARATION OF EXEMPTION

☐ This activity has been reviewed and approved by an IRB in accordance with the requirements of 45 CFR 46, including its relevant Subparts. This certification fulfills, when applicable, requirements for certifying FDA status for each investigational new drug or device *(see reverse side of this form)*.

_____ Date of IRB review and approval. *(If approval is pending, write "pending". Followup certification is required.)*
(month/day/year)

☐ Full Board Review   ☐ Expedited Review

☐ This activity contains multiple projects, some of which have not been reviewed. The IRB has granted approval on condition that all projects covered by 45 CFR 46 will be reviewed and approved before they are initiated and that appropriate further certification *(form HHS 596)* will be submitted.

☐ Human subjects are involved but this activity qualifies for exemption under 46.101(b) in accordance with paragraph _____ *(insert paragraph number of exemption in 46.101(b), 1 through 5)*, but the institution did not designate that exemption on the application.

6. **Each official signing below certifies that the information provided on this form is correct and that each institution assumes responsibility for assuring required future reviews, approvals, and submissions of certification.**

APPLICANT INSTITUTION	COOPERATING INSTITUTION
NAME, ADDRESS, AND TELEPHONE NO.	NAME, ADDRESS, AND TELEPHONE NO.
NAME AND TITLE OF OFFICIAL *(print or type)*	NAME AND TITLE OF OFFICIAL *(print or type)*
SIGNATURE OF OFFICIAL LISTED ABOVE *(and date)*	SIGNATURE OF OFFICIAL LISTED ABOVE *(and date)*

HHS 596 (Rev. 1/82)   *(If additional space is needed, please use reverse side under "Notes.")*

Exhibit 46. Federal Certification Form.

CERTIFICATIONS REGARDING LOBBYING; DEBARMENT, SUSPENSION AND OTHER RESPONSIBILITY MATTERS; AND DRUG-FREE WORKPLACE REQUIREMENTS

Applicants should refer to the regulations cited below to determine the certification to which they are required to attest. Applicants should also review the instructions for certification included in the regulations before completing this form. Signature of this form provides for compliance with certification requirements under 34 CFR Part 82, "New Restrictions on Lobbying," and 34 CFR Part 85, "Government-wide Debarment and Suspension (Nonprocurement) and Government-wide Requirements for Drug-Free Workplace (Grants)." The certifications shall be treated as a material representation of fact upon which reliance will be placed when the Department of Education determines to award the covered transaction, grant, or cooperative agreement.

1. LOBBYING

As required by Section 1352, Title 31 of the U.S. Code, and implemented at 34 CFR Part 82, for persons entering into a grant or cooperative agreement over $100,000, as defined at 34 CFR Part 82, Sections 82.105 and 82.110, the applicant certifies that:

(a) No Federal appropriated funds have been paid or will be paid, by or on behalf of the undersigned, to any person for influencing or attempting to influence an officer or employee of any agency, a Member of Congress, an officer or employee of Congress, or an employee of a Member of Congress in connection with the making of any Federal grant, the entering into of any cooperative agreement, and the extension, continuation, renewal, amendment, or modification of any Federal grant or cooperative agreement;

(b) If any funds other than Federal appropriated funds have been paid or will be paid to any person for influencing or attempting to influence an officer or employee of any agency, a Member of Congress, an officer or employee of Congress, or an employee of a Member of Congress in connection with this Federal grant or cooperative agreement, the undersigned shall complete and submit Standard Form - LLL, "Disclosure Form to Report Lobbying," in accordance with its instructions;

(c) The undersigned shall require that the language of this certification be included in the award documents for all subawards at all tiers (including subgrants, contracts under grants and cooperative agreements, and subcontracts) and that all subrecipients shall certify and disclose accordingly.

2. DEBARMENT, SUSPENSION, AND OTHER RESPONSIBILITY MATTERS

As required by Executive Order 12549, Debarment and Suspension, and implemented at 34 CFR Part 85, for prospective participants in primary covered transactions, as defined at 34 CFR Part 85, Sections 85.105 and 85.110—

A. The applicant certifies that it and its principals:

(a) Are not presently debarred, suspended, proposed for debarment, declared ineligible, or voluntarily excluded from covered transactions by any Federal department or agency;

(b) Have not within a three-year period preceding this application been convicted of or had a civil judgment rendered against them for commission of fraud or a criminal offense in connection with obtaining, attempting to obtain, or performing a public (Federal, State, or local) transaction or contract under a public transaction; violation of Federal or State antitrust statutes or commission of embezzlement, theft, forgery, bribery, falsification or destruction of records, making false statements, or receiving stolen property;

(c) Are not presently indicted for or otherwise criminally or civilly charged by a governmental entity (Federal, State, or local) with commission of any of the offenses enumerated in paragraph (1)(b) of this certification; and

(d) Have not within a three-year period preceding this application had one or more public transactions (Federal, State, or local) terminated for cause or default; and

B. Where the applicant is unable to certify to any of the statements in this certification, he or she shall attach an explanation to this application.

3. DRUG-FREE WORKPLACE (GRANTEES OTHER THAN INDIVIDUALS)

As required by the Drug-Free Workplace Act of 1988, and implemented at 34 CFR Part 85, Subpart F, for grantees, as defined at 34 CFR Part 85, SEctions 85.605 and 85.610—

A. The applicant certifies that it will or will continue to provide a drug-free workplace by:

(a) Publishing a statement notifying employees that the unlawful manufacture, distribution, dispensing, possession, or use of a controlled substance is prohibited in the grantee's workplace and specifying the actions that will be taken against employees for violation of such prohibition;

(b) Establishing an on-going drug-free awareness program to inform employees about—

(1) The dangers of drug abuse in the workplace;

(2) The grantee's policy of maintaining a drug-free workplace;

(3) Any available drug counseling, rehabilitation, and employee assistance programs; and

(4) The penalties that may be imposed upon employees for drug abuse violations occurring in the workplace;

Exhibit 46. Federal Certification Form (cont.).

(c) Making it a requirement that each employee to be engaged in the performance of the grant be given a copy of the statement required by paragraph (a);

(d) Notifying the employee in the statement required by paragraph (a) that, as a condition of employment under the grant, the employee will—

(1) Abide by the terms of the statement; and

(2) Notify the employer in writing of his or her conviction for a violation of a criminal drug statute occurring in the workpalce no later than five calendar days after such conviction;

(e) Notifying the agency, in writing, within 10 calendar days after receiving notice under subparagraph (d)(2) from an employee or otherwise receiving actual notice of such conviction. Employers of convicted employees must provide notice, including position title, to: Director, Grants and Contracts Service, U.S. Department of Education, 400 Maryland Avenue, S.W. (Room 3124, GSA Regional Office Building No. 3), Washington, DC 20202-4571. Notice shall include the identification number(s) of each affected grant;

(f) Taking one of the following actions, within 30 calendar days of receiving notice under subparagraph (d)(2), with respect to any employee who is so convicted—

(1) Taking appropriate personnel action against such an employee, up to and including termination, consistent with the requirements of the Rehabilitation Act of 1973, as amended; or

(2) Requiring such employee to participate satisfactorily in a drug abuse assistance or rehabilitation program approved for such purposes by a Federal, State, or local health, law enforcement, or other appropriate agency;

(g) Making a good faith effort to continue to maintain a drug-free workplace through implementation of paragraphs (a), (b), (c), (d), (e), and (f).

B. The grantee may insert in the space provided below the site(s) for the performance of work done in connection with the specific grant:

Place of Performance (Street address, city, county, state, zip code)

_____

_____

_____

Check □ if there are workplaces on file that are not identified here.

DRUG-FREE WORKPLACE (GRANTEES WHO ARE INDIVIDUALS)

As required by the Drug-Free Workplace Act of 1988, and implemented at 34 CFR Part 85, Subpart F, for grantees, as defined at 34 CFR Part 85, Sections 85.605 and 85.610—

A. As a condition of the grant, I certify that I will not engage in the unlawful manufacture, distribution, dispensing, possession, or use of a controlled substance in conducting any activity with the grant; and

B. If convicted of a criminal drug offense resulting from a violation occurring during the conduct of any grant activity, I will report the conviction, in writing, within 10 calendar days of the conviction, to: Director, Grants and Contracts Service, U.S. Department of Education, 400 Maryland Avenue, S.W. (Room 3124, GSA Regional Office Building No. 3), Washington, DC 20202-4571. Notice shall include the indentification number(s) of each affected grant.

As the duly authorized representative of the applicant, I hereby certify that the applicant will comply with the above certifications.

NAME OF APPLICANT	PR/AWARD NUMBER AND/OR PROJECT NAME
PRINTED NAME AND TITLE OF AUTHORIZED REPRESENTATIVE	
SIGNATURE	DATE

U. S. GOVERNMENT PRINTING OFFICE : 1990 O - 273-448

Exhibit 47. USDA Certification Form.

UNITED STATES DEPARTMENT OF AGRICULTURE

CERTIFICATION REGARDING DEBARMENT, SUSPENSION, AND OTHER RESPONSIBILITY MATTERS - PRIMARY COVERED TRANSACTIONS

This certification is required by the regulations implementing Executive Order 12549, Debarment and Suspension, 7 CFR Part 3017, Section 3017.510, Participants' responsibilities. The regulations were published as Part IV of the January 30, 1989, **Federal Register** (pages 4722-4733). Copies of the regulation may be obtained by contacting the Department of Agriculture agency offering the proposed covered transaction.

(Before completing Certification, read Instructions on reverse)

(1) The prospective primary participant certifies to the best of its knowledge and belief, that it and its principals:

    (a) are not presently debarred, suspended, proposed for debarment, declared ineligible, or voluntarily excluded from covered transactions by any Federal department or agency;

    (b) have not within a three-year period preceding this proposal been convicted of or had a civil judgment rendered against them for commission of fraud or a criminal offense in connection with obtaining, attempting to obtain, or performing a public (Federal, State or Local) transaction or contract under a public transaction; violation of Federal or State antitrust statutes or commission of embezzlement, theft, forgery, bribery, falsification or destruction of records, making false statements, or receiving stolen property;

    (c) are not presently indicted for or otherwise criminally or civilly charged by a governmental entity (Federal, State or Local) with commission of any of the offenses enumerated in paragraph (1)(b) of this certification; and

    (d) have not within a three-year period preceding this application/proposal had one or more public transactions (Federal, State or Local) terminated for cause or default.

(2) Where the prospective primary participant is unable to certify to any of the statements in this certification, such prospective participant shall attach an explanation to this proposal.

Organization Name   PR/Award Number or Project Name

Name and Title of Authorized Representative

Signature   Date

Form AD-1047 (9/89)

Exhibit 48. Disclosure of Lobbying Activities Form.

DISCLOSURE OF LOBBYING ACTIVITIES

Approved by OMB
0348-0046

Complete this form to disclose lobbying activities pursuant to 31 U.S.C. 1352
(See reverse for public burden disclosure.)

1. Type of Federal Action:
 ☐   a. contract
     b. grant
     c. cooperative agreement
     d. loan
     e. loan guarantee
     f. loan insurance
	2. Status of Federal Action:
	 ☐ a. bid/offer/application
	     b. initial award
	     c. post-award
		3. Report Type:
		 ☐ a. initial filing
		     b. material change
		 For Material Change Only:
		    year _____ quarter _____
		    date of last report _____

4. Name and Address of Reporting Entity: ☐ Prime ☐ Subawardee Tier _____ , *if known:* **Congressional District,** *if known:*	**5. If Reporting Entity in No. 4 is Subawardee, Enter Name and Address of Prime:** **Congressional District,** *if known:*
6. Federal Department/Agency:	**7. Federal Program Name/Description:** CFDA Number, *if applicable:* _____
8. Federal Action Number, *if known:*	**9. Award Amount,** *if known:* $
10. a. Name and Address of Lobbying Entity *(if individual, last name, first name, MI):*	**b. Individuals Performing Services** *(including address if different from No. 10a)* *(last name, first name, MI):*

(attach Continuation Sheet(s) SF-LLL-A, if necessary)

11. Amount of Payment *(check all that apply):*
 	
 $ _____   ☐ actual   ☐ planned
 	
 12. Form of Payment *(check all that apply):*
    ☐ a. cash
    ☐ b. in-kind; specify: nature _____
                        value _____
	13. Type of Payment *(check all that apply):*
	    ☐ a. retainer
	    ☐ b. one-time fee
	    ☐ c. commission
	    ☐ d. contingent fee
	    ☐ e. deferred
	    ☐ f. other; specify: _____

14. Brief Description of Services Performed or to be Performed and Date(s) of Service, including officer(s), employee(s), or Member(s) contacted, for Payment Indicated in Item 11:

(attach Continuation Sheet(s) SF-LLL-A, if necessary)

15. Continuation Sheet(s) SF-LLL-A attached: ☐ Yes   ☐ No

16. Information requested through this form is authorized by title 31 U.S.C. section 1352. This disclosure of lobbying activities is a material representation of fact upon which reliance was placed by the tier above when this transaction was made or entered into. This disclosure is required pursuant to 31 U.S.C. 1352. This information will be reported to the Congress semi-annually and will be available for public inspection. Any person who fails to file the required disclosure shall be subject to a civil penalty of not less than $10,000 and not more than $100,000 for each such failure.	Signature: _____ Print Name: _____ Title: _____ Telephone No.: _____ Date: _____

Federal Use Only:	Authorized for Local Reproduction Standard Form - LLL

27

Exhibit 48. Disclosure of Lobbying Activities Form (cont.).

INSTRUCTIONS FOR COMPLETION OF SF-LLL, DISCLOSURE OF LOBBYING ACTIVITIES

This disclosure form shall be completed by the reporting entity, whether subawardee or prime Federal recipient, at the initiation or receipt of a covered Federal action, or a material change to a previous filing, pursuant to title 31 U.S.C. section 1352. The filing of a form is required for each payment or agreement to make payment to any lobbying entity for influencing or attempting to influence an officer or employee of any agency, a Member of Congress, an officer or employee of Congress, or an employee of a Member of Congress in connection with a covered Federal action. Use the SF-LLL-A Continuation Sheet for additional information if the space on the form is inadequate. Complete all items that apply for both the initial filing and material change report. Refer to the implementing guidance published by the Office of Management and Budget for additional information.

1. Identify the type of covered Federal action for which lobbying activity is and/or has been secured to influence the outcome of a covered Federal action.

2. Identify the status of the covered Federal action.

3. Identify the appropriate classification of this report. If this is a followup report caused by a material change to the information previously reported, enter the year and quarter in which the change occurred. Enter the date of the last previously submitted report by this reporting entity for this covered Federal action.

4. Enter the full name, address, city, state and zip code of the reporting entity. Include Congressional District, if known. Check the appropriate classification of the reporting entity that designates if it is, or expects to be, a prime or subaward recipient. Identify the tier of the subawardee, e.g., the first subawardee of the prime is the 1st tier. Subawards include but are not limited to subcontracts, subgrants and contract awards under grants.

5. If the organization filing the report in item 4 checks "Subawardee", then enter the full name, address, city, state and zip code of the prime Federal recipient. Include Congressional District, if known.

6. Enter the name of the Federal agency making the award or loan commitment. Include at least one organizational level below agency name, if known. For example, Department of Transportation, United States Coast Guard.

7. Enter the Federal program name or description for the covered Federal action (item 1). If known, enter the full Catalog of Federal Domestic Assistance (CFDA) number for grants, cooperative agreements, loans, and loan commitments.

8. Enter the most appropriate Federal identifying number available for the Federal action identified in item 1 (e.g., Request for Proposal (RFP) number; Invitation for Bid (IFB) number; grant announcement number; the contract, grant, or loan award number; the application/proposal control number assigned by the Federal agency). Include prefixes, e.g., "RFP-DE-90-001."

9. For a covered Federal action where there has been an award or loan commitment by the Federal agency, enter the Federal amount of the award/loan commitment for the prime entity identified in item 4 or 5.

10. (a) Enter the full name, address, city, state and zip code of the lobbying entity engaged by the reporting entity identified in item 4 to influence the covered Federal action.

    (b) Enter the full names of the individual(s) performing services, and include full address if different from 10 (a). Enter Last Name, First Name, and Middle Initial (MI).

11. Enter the amount of compensation paid or reasonably expected to be paid by the reporting entity (item 4) to the lobbying entity (item 10). Indicate whether the payment has been made (actual) or will be made (planned). Check all boxes that apply. If this is a material change report, enter the cumulative amount of payment made or planned to be made.

12. Check the appropriate box(es). Check all boxes that apply. If payment is made through an in-kind contribution, specify the nature and value of the in-kind payment.

13. Check the appropriate box(es). Check all boxes that apply. If other, specify nature.

14. Provide a specific and detailed description of the services that the lobbyist has performed, or will be expected to perform, and the date(s) of any services rendered. Include all preparatory and related activity, not just time spent in actual contact with Federal officials. Identify the Federal official(s) or employee(s) contacted or the officer(s), employee(s), or Member(s) of Congress that were contacted.

15. Check whether or not a SF-LLL-A Continuation Sheet(s) is attached.

16. The certifying official shall sign and date the form, print his/her name, title, and telephone number.

Public reporting burden for this collection of information is estimated to average 30 mintues per response, including time for reviewing instructions, searching existing data sources, gathering and maintaining the data needed, and completing and reviewing the collection of information. Send comments regarding the burden estimate or any other aspect of this collection of information, including suggestions for reducing this burden, to the Office of Management and Budget, Paperwork Reduction Project (0348-0046), Washington, D.C. 20503.

28

Exhibit 49. Certification Regarding Drug-free Workplace Requirements other than Individuals.

Certification Regarding Drug-Free Workplace Requirements
Grantees Other Than Individuals

This certification is required by the regulations implementing the Drug-Free Workplace Act of 1988, 34 CFR Part 85, Subpart F. The regulations, published in the January 31, 1989 *Federal Register,* require certification by grantees, prior to award, that they will maintain a drug-free workplace. The certification set out below is a material representation of fact upon which reliance will be placed when the agency determines to award the grant. False certification or violation of the certification shall be grounds for suspension of payments, suspension or termination of grants, or governmentwide suspension or debarment (see 34 CFR Part 85, Sections 85.615 and 85.620).

The grantee certifies that it will provide a drug-free workplace by:

(a) Publishing a statement notifying employees that the unlawful manufacture, distribution, dispensing, possession or use of a controlled substance is prohibited in the grantee's workplace and specifying the actions that will be taken against employees for violation of such prohibition;

(b) Establishing a drug-free awareness program to inform employees about—

   (1) The dangers of drug abuse in the workplace;
   (2) The grantee's policy of maintaining a drug-free workplace;
   (3) Any available drug counseling, rehabilitation, and employee assistance programs; and
   (4) The penalties that may be imposed upon employees for drug abuse violations occurring in the workplace;

(c) Making it a requirement that each employee to be engaged in the performance of the grant be given a copy of the statement required by paragraph (a);

(d) Notifying the employee in the statement required by paragraph (a) that, as a condition of employment under the grant, the employee will—

   (1) Abide by the terms of the statement; and
   (2) Notify the employer of any criminal drug statute conviction for a violation occurring in the workplace no later than five days after such conviction;

(e) Notifying the agency within ten days after receiving notice under subparagraph (d)(2) from an employee or otherwise receiving actual notice of such conviction;

(f) Taking one of the following actions, within 30 days of receiving notice under subparagraph (d)(2), with respect to any employee who is so convicted—

   (1) Taking appropriate personnel action against such an employee, up to and including termination; or
   (2) Requiring such employee to participate satisfactorily in a drug abuse assistance or rehabilitation program approved for such purposes by a Federal, State, or local health, law enforcement, or other appropriate agency;

(g) Making a good faith effort to continue to maintain a drug-free workplace through implementation of paragraphs (a), (b), (c), (d), (e) and (f).

Organization Name   PR/Award Number or Project Name

Name and Title of Authorized Representative

Signature   Date

ED 80-0004

5. Sample Drug-Free Workplace Policy Statement

Exhibit 50. Drug-Free Workplace Statement.

CURI
COLLEGE-UNIVERSITY RESOURCE INSTITUTE, INC.
1001 CONNECTICUT AVE., N.W. • SUITE 901 • WASHINGTON, D.C. 20036 • (202) 659-2104

To: All Employees and Board of Directors

From: Julie A. Thompsen

Date: April 28, 1989

Subject: Drug Free Workplace Act

On October 22, 1988, Congress passed the omnibus Anti-Drug Abuse Act of 1988 which included ratification of the Drug Free Workplace Act of 1988. The Drug Free Workplace Act, which was signed into law by President Reagan on November 18, 1988, and becomes effective March 18, 1989, requires all institutions who receive Federal grants to institute affirmative programs designed to prevent "employees from manufacturing, possessing, or using illegal drugs." CURI receives federal grants and, therefore, must comply with the Drug Free Workplace Act. Failure to comply with the Act can result in suspension of payments of grants and/or non-approval of future grants.

Although the Department of Education has yet to send us detailed information, compliance with the Act is concentrated in four general areas.

1. Reaffirmation of an institution's policies towards drug abuse.

2. The establishment of a drug-free awareness program within the work-place.

3. The availability of drug counseling, rehabilitation, and employee assistance programs.

4. The proper reporting of any violations that do occur within the workplace.

All of us will be hearing a great deal more about the Drug Free Workplace Act in the near future. I do think it is imperative, however, for CURI at this time to reaffirm its position concerning controlled substance abuse in our organization.

The unlawful manufacture, distribution, dispensing, possession or use of controlled substance is prohibited in the workplace. Failure to comply will lead to dismissal.

Information on the danger of drugs is available to all CURI employees. Informal dangerous drug use discussions are held in the office.

Employees will be assisted in finding appropriate counselling services as appropriate.

No employee will report to work while under the influence of alcohol or illegal drugs. Violation of these rules will be reason for mandatory evaulation/treatment for a substance use disorder or for disciplinary action up to and including removal.

An employee convicted of any criminal drug statute occuring in the workplace must notify the employer (CURI) no later than 5 days after such conviction.

CURI will notify any Federal contracting agency within 10 days of receiving notice that an employee engaged in the performance of such contract has had any criminal drug statute violation occuring in the workplace.

This policy statement is sent to every employee of CURI as our good faith effort to maintain a drug free workplace.

Thank you for your cooperation and understanding in this matter.

6. An IRS Letter of Determination

Exhibit 51. IRS Letter of Determination.

Internal Revenue Service District Director	Department of the Treasury

Date: February 16, 1983

521244583
Employer Identification Number:
December 31
Accounting Period Ending:
509(a)(2)
Foundation Status Classification:
Dec. 31, 1986
Advance Ruling Period Ends:

▷ College University Resource
Institute, Inc.

Person to Contact: Taxpayer Service
Division
Contact Telephone Number:
488-3100

Dear Applicant:

Based on information supplied, and assuming your operations will be as stated
in your application for recognition of exemption, we have determined you are exempt
from Federal income tax under section 501(c)(3) of the Internal Revenue Code.

Because you are a newly created organization, we are not now making a final
determination of your foundation status under section 509(a) of the Code. However,
we have determined that you can reasonably be expected to be a publicly supported
organization described in section   509(a)(2)

Accordingly, you will be treated as a publicly supported organization, and not
as a private foundation, during an advance ruling period. This advance ruling period
begins on the date of your inception and ends on the date shown above.

Within 90 days after the end of your advance ruling period, you must submit to
us information needed to determine whether you have met the requirements of the
applicable support test during the advance ruling period. If you establish that you
have been a publicly supported organization, you will be classified as a section
509(a)(1) or 509(a)(2) organization as long as you continue to meet the requirements
of the applicable support test. If you do not meet the public support requirements
during the advance ruling period, you will be classified as a private foundation for
future periods. Also, if you are classified as a private foundation, you will be
treated as a private foundation from the date of your inception for purposes of
sections 507(d) and 4940.

Grantors and donors may rely on the determination that you are not a private
foundation until 90 days after the end of your advance ruling period. If you submit
the required information within the 90 days, grantors and donors may continue to
rely on the advance determination until the Service makes a final determination of
your foundation status. However, if notice that you will no longer be treated as a
section 509(a)(2)   organization is published in the Internal Revenue Bulletin,
grantors and donors may not rely on this determination after the date of such
publication. Also, a grantor or donor may not rely on this determination if he or
she was in part responsible for, or was aware of, the act or failure to act that
resulted in your loss of section 509(a)(2)   status, or acquired knowledge that
the Internal Revenue Service had given notice that you would be removed from
classification as a section 509(a)(2)   organization.

If your gross receipts each year are normally more than $5,000,
you are required to file Form 990, Return of Organization Exempt
From Income Tax, by the 15th day of the fifth month after the end
of your annual accounting period. The law imposes a penalty of $10
a day, up to a maximum of $5,000, for failure to file a return on time.

You are not required to file Federal income tax returns unless
you are subject to the tax on unrelated business income under section
511 of the Code. If you are subject to this tax, you must file an income
tax return on Form 990-T. In this letter we are not determining whether
any of your present or proposed activities are unrelated trade or
business as defined in section 513 of the Code.

You need an employer identification number even if you have no
employees. If an employer identification number was not entered on
your application, a number will be assigned to you and you will be
advised of it. Please use that number on all returns you file and in
all correspondence with the Internal Revenue Service.

Please keep this determination letter in your permanent records.

Sincerely yours,

Gerald G. Portney

Gerald G. Portney
District Director

P. O. Box 13163, Baltimore, MD 21203

Letter 1045(DO) (6—77)

Section V. Annotated Bibliography

The following annotated bibliography is not intended to be comprehensive. It is an attempt to provide a sampling of sources of information regarding the process of grant seeking and grant administration. The prices and addresses are always subject to change. We have included only those publications with which we are familiar and realize that there are undoubtedly other sources of comparable value that you may want to add to the list.

Considerable attention has been given to the Foundation Center publications because this nonprofit organization offers the most comprehensive information and service on private foundations. The Foundation Center operates public reference libraries in New York City and Washington, DC, with field offices in Cleveland and San Francisco, and maintains collections in numerous libraries throughout the United States. The national offices will gladly give you information on the location of these collections. Write, call, or FAX your request to one of the following locations:

> The Foundation Center
> 79 Fifth Avenue
> New York, NY 10003
> (212) 620-4230
> FAX (212) 691-1828
>
> or
>
> The Foundation Center
> 1001 Connecticut Avenue, NW
> Washington, DC 20036
> (202) 331-1400
> FAX (202) 331-1739

The most essential and basic publications for federal sources of support and grant administration requirements are the *Catalog of Federal Domestic Assistance* and the *Federal Register*. Though there are many good commercial newsletters and information services covering government sources, the government is the original source for its information, and this information, when secured directly from an agency or the Government Printing Office (GPO), costs little or is free in many cases.

The compilations and analyses of grant opportunities by independent organizations and experts are costly. Learn all you can from the Foundation Center and direct federal sources, then test and choose other publications wisely. Examine any costly publication before subscribing to it.

ALA Washington Newsletter — Monthly
American Library Association — $25.00/year
110 Maryland Avenue, NE
Washington, DC 20002
(202) 547-4440
> Coverage of and commentary on the status of library programs with regard to legislation and funding. A timely and accurate publication.

Annual Register of Grant Support — Updated Annually
Marquis Academic Media — $85.00 plus
Marquis Who's Who, Inc. — postage
4300 West 62nd Street
Indianapolis, IN 46268
(317) 298-5496
> A compendium of 1500 grant support programs of government agencies, public and private foundations, business and industrial firms, unions, educational and professional associations, and special interest organizations.

Catalog of Federal Domestic Assistance — Annually (near
Superintendent of Documents — the start of FY)
U.S. Government Printing Office — $35.00
Washington, DC 20402
(202) 783-3228
> A cross-indexed directory of all federal programs. Listed are the agency, funding authorization, legislative reference, program description, and the contact person. Regional offices and agency addresses are included. The programs are classified according to a standard numbering system. The *Catalog* is an essential part of the library of any institution or organization with any interest in government programs (Depository Item 853-A-1).

The Chronicle of Higher Education — 48 issues/year
1255 23rd Street, N.W. — $62.50/year
Washington, DC 20037
(202) 466-1000
Send subscription to:

The Chronicle
Box 1989
Marion, OH 43305
(202) 828-3500 or 1-800-347-6969

A "must" for weekly coverage (during the academic year) of the campus issues, the Washington scene, personnel changes in higher education, and major grant awards. *The Chronicle* is noted for its accuracy and fairness.

The Chronicle of Philanthropy $57.50/year
1255 23rd Street, N.W.
Washington, DC 20037
(202) 466-1200

A "must" for charities and nonprofits. Relatively new publication with excellent and current information on funding sources: corporate, private, and government. (Like its counterpart *Higher Ed*, it is known for accuracy.)

Commerce Business Daily   Daily
Superintendent of Documents $208.00/year
U.S. Government Printing Office
(202) 783-3238

Federal contract information and RFPs (Request for Proposals) in addition to notice of sales of surplus property and foreign business opportunities. Available in Electronic Edition.

Congressional Record   Daily while Congress is in session
Superintendent of Documents $225.00/year
U.S. Government Printing Office
Washington, DC 20402
(202) 783-3238

Daily proceedings of the House and Senate with all material added for the written record. Subscription or ready access in library essential, depending on the focus of your job.

The Congressional Yellow Book $175.00/year
The Washington Monitor
499 National Press Building
Washington, DC 20045
(202) 347-7757

A directory of Members of Congress, their committees, and their key staff aides. Updated four times per year.

The CFAE Casebook   About $20.00
Council for Financial Aid to Education   price changes
680 Fifth Avenue   with new issue
New York, NY 10019
(212) 541-4050

Coverage of business and corporate programs for support of higher education.

Depository Libraries   Free
U.S. Government Printing Office
Public Documents Department
Washington, DC 20402
(202) 783-3238

Directory of Educational Associations $7.50/year
Superintendent of Documents
U.S. Government Printing Office
Washington, DC 20402
(202) 783-3238

A list of names and addresses of education associations in the United States, their chief officer, and any official publications.

Directory of Research Grants $118/year
The Oryx Press
4041 North Central at Indian School Road
Phoenix, AZ 85012-3397
(602) 265-2651

Nearly 6000 grants available through federal, state, and local governments; foundations; educational institutions; private donors; corporations; religious organizations; and labor unions. This annual directory is part of the GRANTS database, which describes over 8500 funding sources. The GRANTS database is available electronically, both online and on CD-ROM, from Dialog, Inc. Other specialized print directories from the GRANTS family include the *Directory of Grants in the Humanities* and the *Directory of Biomedical and Health Care Grants*.

Education Daily   Daily
Capitol Publications, Inc. $524.00/year
P.O. Box 1453
Alexandria, VA 22313
(703) 683-4100

Accurate daily overview of activities in full range of education interests. If federal government vis-a-vis education is a main interest—a must.

Federal Executive Directory   6 issues per year
Carroll Publishing Company $173.00/year
1058 Thomas Jefferson Street, NW $111.00/single issue
(202) 333-8620

Indexed by agency and by name of individual. Individuals are assigned locator numbers corresponding to agency listing.

Federal Grants and Contracts Weekly   Weekly
Capitol Publications, Inc.   329.00/year
1101 King Street
Alexandria, VA 22314
(703) 683-4100

A newsletter with information on research policy and selected listing of current RFPs. This is one of several specialized newsletters such as *Health Grant & Contracts Weekly*. Further information on these publications may be obtained from Capitol Publications.

Federal Register   Daily (Mon.-Fri.)
Superintendent of Documents $340.00/year
U.S. Government Printing Office $1.50 single issue
Washington, DC 20402
(202) 783-3238

All regulations and proposed rule changes must be published in the *Federal Register*. If you miss seeing it in the Register, you may have missed your last chance to comment or object. Subscription or convenient access to a library with the *Federal Register* is a "must" if you are involved with grants and contracts with the government. The *Federal Register* runs an excellent and free training program on how to use the document.

Federal Research Report　　　　　　50 weeks
Business Publishers　　　　　　　　　$170.00
P.O. Box 1067　　　　　　　　　$12.50 postage
Silver Spring, MD 20910
(301) 587-6300

Commentary on federal activities with government programs, with list of deadlines. One of several similar newsletters. It is more program than legislation-oriented, concise and useful. Deadlines are useful, but double check dates.

The Federal Yellow Book　　　　　$175.00/year
The Washington Monitor
499 National Press Building
Washington, DC 20045
(202) 347-7757

A directory of federal departments and agencies. Names of persons go deep enough in organization to make it very useful. Directory listings are all by agency. Updated throughout the year.

The Foundation Center　the cost of publications varies
79 Fifth Avenue
New York, NY 10003
1-800-424-9836 (In New York State call 212-620-4230)

The Foundation Center is the best single source of information on private foundations. Write or contact the Center for information on current publications and services not in this bibliography.

Foundation Center National Data Book　$125.00/year
79 Fifth Avenue　　　　　　　　　2 volume set
New York, NY 10003
1-800-424-9836 (In New York State call 212-620-4230)

Annual listing of all active grant-making foundations in the United States. Foundations are listed by state in descending order of total grants. Entries include name, address, principal officers, assets, gifts received, total grants. There is an alphabetical index in a separate volume.

Foundation Center Source　　Annual subscription
　Book Profiles　　　　　　　90-91/$650.00
79 Fifth Avenue　　　　　　　One year $350.00
New York, NY 10003
1-800-424-9836 (In New York State call 212-620-4230)

Source Book Profiles offers an in-depth picture of the 1,000 largest foundations, breaking down each one's giving by subject area, type of support, and type of recipient. Service operates on a two year publishing cycle. Five hundred profiles per series are issued bi-monthly.

Foundation Directory　　　　$165.00/Hard Cover
79 Fifth Avenue　　　　　　　$140.00/Soft Cover
New York, NY 10003
(800) 424-9838

Descriptions of the largest United States foundations with assets of $1,000,000 or more and/or annual giving of $100,000 or more—source of 92% of total grant dollars. Listed alphabetically by state, each entry includes foundation purpose and activities, contact person, officers and directors, financial data, application procedures, and telephone numbers when available. Indexes include: geographic, subject, donors, trustees, administrators.

Foundation Grants Index　　　　　$95.00/year
79 Fifth Avenue
New York, NY 10003
(800) 424-9838

Annual volume. The current edition includes over 25,000 grants made by more than 500 major foundations and an expanded analytical introduction. Indexes by key words and phrases, recipients names, subject and geographic location, and grant recipients by population group.

Foundation News including Grants Index　Bimonthly
Council on Foundations, Inc.　　　　　$29.50/year
1828 L Street, NW
Washington, DC 20036
(202) 466-6512

A publication covering the activities of foundations. Includes Grants Index listing, recent foundation grants of $5,000 or more.

Government Organization Manual　　　$15.00/year
Superintendent of Documents
U.S. Government Printing Office
Washington, DC 20402
(202) 783-3238

Describes and charts organization of agencies and lists top officials. Not expensive and is a must after a change of administration.

Grants:How to Find Out About Them and　　Book
What to Do Next　　　　　　　　about $21.00
Plenum Press
227 West 17th Street
New York, NY 10011

Virginia White's book is a complete and well-written treatise by a successful practitioner.

Higher Education Directory Colleges and Universities
Higher Education Publications, Inc.　　　$41/year
6400 Arlington Blvd. #648
Falls Church, VA 22042
(703) 532 2300

A compilation of information on accredited institutions in the United States that offer at least a one-year program of college-level studies. Included are the mailing address, telephone number, identification code, names of chief administrative officers, total enrollment, and basic student charges.

Higher Education Directory $6.00
CASE
11 Dupont Circle, NW Suite 400
Washington, DC 20036
(202) 328-5000

Lists Washington-based higher education associations and affiliated organizations with names and titles of key personnel, addresses, phone and FAX numbers, and descriptions of each group's major activities.

Humanities $15.00
Superintendent of Documents
U.S. Government Printing Office
Washington, DC 20402
(202) 783-3238

A publication that covers interests, activities, and programs of the Endowment. It includes articles by distinguished scholars, discussion of humanities issues, and awards lists in all NEH programs.

Lutheran Resources Commission (LRC-W) 65.00/year
Washington Newsbriefs monthly
Lutheran Resources Commission Washington
5 Thomas Circle, NW
Washington, DC 20005
(202) 667-9844

Extensive, current, and accurate coverage of government programs, private philanthropy, and recent publications and meetings. The information is arranged according to area of interest (e.g., Education, Resource Development, Health, Children, Women).

News, Notes and Deadlines 6 issues/year
Association of College & University Offices $60.00/year
1001 Connecticut Avenue Suite 901
Washington, DC 20036
(202) 659-2104

An accurate and current newsletter containing news of federal and private and foundation grant programs, application deadlines, and grant notices selected for interests of subscriber institutions. Material checked with source prior to publication.

NIH Guide for Grants and Contracts Periodically
Grants and Contracts Guide Distribution Center Free

National Institutes of Health
Room B3BN10, Building 31
Bethesda, MD 20205

A newsletter in loose-leaf format published at irregular intervals to announce scientific initiatives and to provide policy and administrative information on opportunities, requirements, and changes in grants and contracts activities.

NSF Bulletin Monthly
National Science Foundation (except July & August)
Public Information Branch Free
1800 G Street, NW Room 531
Washington, DC 20550
(202) 357-7861

A bulletin that gives program deadlines and contains information about new programs and other NSF activities (hearings, conferences, etc.). A publications order form on the last page can make obtaining program materials an easier task. Always double check the program deadlines.

Philanthropic Digest $79.50/year
66 Old Kings Highway
Wilton, CT 06897

News and lists of awards by private philanthropy to education, health, religion, welfare and the arts.

Public Health Service Grants Free
(Policy Statement) available
Public Health Service upon request
Grants Management Branch Office, Resource Mgmt.
Room 18A-03, Parklawn Building
5600 Fishers Lane
Rockville, MD 20852
(301) 443-1874

The PHS policies governing the awarding of grants and their subsequent administration.

Washington International Arts Letter 10 issues/year
P.O. Box 12010 $124.00/year
Des Moines, IA 50312
(515) 255-5577

A newsletter that contains information pertinent to the arts, humanities, and education (with emphasis on the arts), including foundation programs, government activities and publication.

Index

by Linda Webster

AAAS. *See* American Association for Advancement of Science (AAAS)

AAC. *See* Association of American Colleges (AAC)

AACJC. *See* American Association of Community and Junior Colleges (AACJC)

AACN. *See* American Association of Colleges of Nursing (AACN)

AACSB. *See* American Assembly of Collegiate School of Business (AACSB)

AACTE. *See* American Association of Colleges for Teacher Education (AACTE)

AAHE. *See* American Association for Higher Education (AAHE)

AALS. *See* Association of American Law Schools (AALS)

AAMC. *See* Association of American Medical Colleges (AAMC)

AASCU. *See* American Association of State Colleges and Universities (AASCU)

AAU. *See* Association of American Universities (AAU)

AAUP. *See* American Association of University Professors (AAUP)

AAUW. *See* American Association of University Women (AAUW)

Abstract, 13-14

Academic Dean, 8

ACE. *See* American Council on Education (ACE)

Acknowledgment card, 117

ACS. *See* American Chemical Society (ACS)

Activity schedule/status report, 9, 11

ACUO. *See* Association of College and University Offices, Inc. (ACUO)

Administration. *See* Grant administration

AGB. *See* Association of Government Boards of Universities and Colleges (AGB)

AHC. *See* Association of Academic Health Centers (AHC)

AJCU. *See* Association of Jesuit Colleges and Universities (AJCU)

ALA Washington Newsletter, 130

Alfred P. Sloan Foundation, 31

American Assembly of Collegiate School of Business (AACSB), 72

American Association for Advancement of Science (AAAS), 72

American Association for Higher Education (AAHE), 71

American Association of Colleges for Teacher Education (AACTE), 71

American Association of Colleges of Nursing (AACN), 71

American Association of Community and Junior Colleges (AACJC), 71

American Association of State Colleges and Universities (AASCU), 14, 71

American Association of University Professors (AAUP), 72

American Association of University Women (AAUW), 72

American Chemical Society (ACS), 72

American Council on Education (ACE), 71

American Society for Engineering Education (ASEE), 71

American Society of Allied Health Professions (ASAHP), 71

Annual Register of Grant Support, 130

APPA. *See* Association of Physical Plant Administrators of Universities and Colleges (APPA)

Appendix, 21

ASAHP. *See* American Society of Allied Health Professions (ASAHP)

ASEE. *See* American Society for Engineering Education (ASEE)

Association of Academic Health Centers (AHC), 72

Association of American Colleges (AAC), 72

Association of American Law Schools (AALS), 72

Association of American Medical Colleges (AAMC), 71

Association of American Universities (AAU), 71

Association of Catholic Colleges and Universities, 71

Association of College and University Offices, Inc. (ACUO), 72

Association of Government Boards of Universities and Colleges (AGB), 71

Association of Jesuit Colleges and Universities (AJCU), 72

Association of Physical Plant Administrators of Universities and Colleges (APPA), 72

Association of University Programs in Health Administration (AUPHA), 71

Assurances
Civil Rights Certificate, 120
Debarment, Suspension, and Other Responsibility Matters, 122, 124
Drug-Free Workplace Requirements, 122-23, 127-28
list of required assurances, 119
Lobbying Activities, 122, 125-26
Protection of Human Subjects Assurance, 121

AUPHA. *See* Association of University Programs in Health Administration (AUPHA)

Budget
review criteria for, 26
sample budget, 19-20
sample revised budget, 42-43
section in proposal, 19

CASE. *See* Council for Advancement and Support of Education (CASE)

Catalog of Federal Domestic Assistance, 30, 69, 130

CFAE Casebook, 131

CGS. *See* Council of Graduate Schools in the U.S. (CGS)

Chronicle, The, 131

Chronicle of Higher Education, 130

Chronicle of Philanthropy, The, 131

CIC. *See* Council of Independent Colleges (CIC)

CIES. *See* Council for International Exchange of Scholars (CIES)

Civil Rights Certificate, 120

CLR. *See* Council on Library Resources, Inc. (CLR)

College and University Personnel
Association (CUPA), 72
Commerce Business Daily, 131
Congressional Record, 131
Congressional Yellow Book, 131
"Cost-sharing," 19
Council for Advancement and Support of
Education (CASE), 71
Council for International Exchange of
Scholars (CIES), 72
Council of Graduate Schools in the U.S.
(CGS), 71
Council of Independent Colleges (CIC),
71
Council on Library Resources, Inc.
(CLR), 72
Cover sheet, 13, 32, 41
CUPA. *See* College and University
Personnel Association (CUPA)
Curriculum vitae, 116

Debarment, Suspension, and Other
Responsibility Matters, Certification
Regarding, 122, 124
Department Chair, 8
Department members, 8
Department of Agriculture
forms, 108-10, 124
news releases from, 69
Department of Defense, 74-79
Department of Education
forms, 80-81
news releases from, 69
Department of Energy, 69
Department of Health and Human
Services
forms, 82-85
news releases from, 69
Department of Labor, 69
Department of Transportation, 69
Depository Libraries, 131
Directory of Educational Associations,
131
Directory of Research Grants, 31, 69, 131
Dissemination, section in proposal, 18
DOE. *See* Department of Energy
DOL. *See* Department of Labor
DOT. *See* Department of Transportation
Drug-Free Workplace Requirements,
Certification Regarding, 122-23,
127-28

ED. *See* Department of Education
Education Daily, 131
Educational Resources Information
Center Clearinghouse on Higher
Education (ERIC/HE), 71
Educational Resources Information
Center Clearinghouse on Teacher
Education (ERIC/TE), 71
Endorsement letters, 32-33
Environmental Protection Agency, 69
EPA. *See* Environmental Protection
Agency

ERIC/HE. *See* Educational Resources
Information Center Clearinghouse on
Higher Education (ERIC/HE)
ERIC/TE. *See* Educational Resources
Information Center Clearinghouse on
Teacher Education (ERIC/TE)
Evaluation
agency requirement for, 49-50
example evaluation, 50-62
formative evaluation, 21
of grant proposal, 21-29
importance of, 49
preparation of effective evaluation plan, 50
of project, 16, 18
summative evaluation, 21

Facilities, section in proposal, 18
Federal Executive Directory, 131
Federal Grants and Contracts Weekly,
131
Federal Register, 31, 69, 130, 131-32
Federal Research Report, 132
FIPSE. *See* Fund for Improvement of Post
Secondary Education (FIPSE)
Fiscal Officer, 8, 35-36
Formative evaluation, 21
Forms
acknowledgment card, 117
certification and assurance forms
and regulations, 118-29
Civil Rights Certificate, 120
curriculum vitae, 116
Debarment, Suspension, and
Other Responsibility Matters,
122, 124
Department of Agriculture, 108-
10
Department of Defense, 74-79
Department of Education, 80-81
Department of Health and Human
Services, 82-85
Drug-Free Workplace Require-
ments, 122-23, 127-28
foundations, 111-15
Lobbying Activities, 122, 125-26
National Endowment for the Arts,
86-96
National Endowment for the
Humanities, 97-103
National Science Foundation,
104-07
Protection of Human Subjects
Assurance, 121
Foundation Center, 72, 130, 132
Foundation Center National Data Book,
132
Foundation Center Source Book Profiles,
132
Foundation Directory, 31, 69, 132
Foundation Grants Index, 132
Foundation Library, 31
Foundation News including Grants Index,
132

Foundations
forms, 111-15
as funding source, 31
rejection of proposals, 37
Fund for Improvement of Post Secondary
Education (FIPSE), 50

Goals and objectives, 15
Government Organization Manual, 132
Government Printing Office (GPO), 70,
130
GPO. *See* Government Printing Office
(GPO)
GPO Bookstore, 70
Grant administration
case study, 37-48
checklist for, 36
communication from and with the
sponsor, 35
negotiation and acceptance of
grant, 36-37
preparation for securing and
expending grant funds, 35-36
rejection/self-appraisal/
resubmission of grant, 37
Grant proposal. *See also* names of
specific agencies
abstract for, 13-14
activity schedule/status report for
develoment of ideas, 9, 11
appendix for, 21
budget for, 19-20, 26, 42-43
clear writing for, 15-16
components of, 12, 13-21
cover sheet for, 13, 32, 41
criteria for review of, 22-29
dissemination section in, 18
evaluation section for, 16, 18, 49-
50
facilities section in, 18
final check of, 34
finding a source for support, 30-
31
and following instructions, 34
general considerations for, 12-13
goals and objectives for, 15
information sources on, 69-72,
130-33
letter of transmittal for, 33, 40
letters of endorsement for, 32-33
list of activities for, 16
negotiation and acceptance of,
36-37
Originator's role and responsibilities in, 6-8, 30-31
personnel section for, 18-19
problem statement for, 14
procedures section for, 15
rejection/self-appraisal/
resubmission of, 37
review process for, 21-29
sample budget, 42-43
sample cover sheet, 41
sample letters of transmittal, 40

Grant proposal *(continued)*
    sample review criteria, 23-29
    shortcomings found in, 28-29
    sources of assistance and
        training, 71-72
    submission of, 32-34
    table of contents for, 13
    timetable for development of, 9,
        10
    types of grant applications, 74
    typical responses from sponsor,
        35
    typing requirements for, 33-34
GRANTS (database), 131
*Grants: How to Find Out About Them
    and What to Do Next,* 132
Grants/Sponsored Programs Officer
    finding a source of support, 30-31
    and negotiation and acceptance of
        grant, 37
    and preparation for securing and
        expending grant funds, 35
    role and responsibilities of, 8-9

HEPALIS. *See* Higher Education Policy
    and Administration Library and
    Information Service (HEPALIS)
HHS. *See* Department of Health and
    Human Services
Higher Education Directory (CASE), 133
*Higher Education Directory Colleges and
    Universities,* 132
Higher Education Policy and Administra-
    tion Library and Information Service
    (HEPALIS), 71
Hightower, John, 15
Human Subjects, Protection of, 121
Humanities, 69, 133

ICET. *See* International Council on
    Education (ICET)
Ideas
    Academic Dean's role and
        responsibilities in, 8
    activity schedule/status report for
        develoment of, 9, 11
    Department Chair's role and
        responsibilities in, 8
    department members' role and
        responsibilities in, 8
    development of, 6
    feedback relation between
        institution and, 3-4
    Fiscal Officer's role and
        responsibilities in, 8
    Grants/Sponsored Programs
        Officer's role and responsi-
        bilities in, 8-9
    institution's role and responsibil-
        ity in, 6
    method for helping ideas to serve
        institutions, 4
    origin and early development of,
        6-11
    Originator's role and responsi-
        bilities in, 6-8

people involved in development
    of ideas, 7-9
    President/Chancellor's role and
        reponsibilities in, 8
    system of development for, 9-11
    timetable for, 9, 10
Information sources, 69-72, 130-33
Institutions. *See* Nonprofit institutions
Internal Revenue Service
    definition of nonprofit institution,
        4-5
    Letter of Determination, 129
International Council on Education
    (ICET), 72
IRS. *See* Internal Revenue Service

Lancaster, Sherry, 50
Law School Admission Council (LSAC),
    71
Letter of transmittal, 33, 40
Letters of endorsement, 32-33
Lobbying Activities, Disclosure of, 122,
    125-26
LRC-W. *See* Lutheran Resources
    Commission (LRC- W)
LSAC. *See* Law School Admission
    Council (LSAC)
Lutheran Resources Commission
    (LRC-W), 72
*Lutheran Resources Commission (LRC-
    W) Washington Newsbriefs,* 133

"Matching" money, 19

NACUA. *See* National Association of
    College and University Attorneys
    (NACUA)
NACUBO. *See* National Association of
    College and University Business
    Officers (NACUBO)
NAFEO. *See* National Association for
    Equal Opportunity in Higher
    Education (NAFEO)
NAICU. *See* National Association of
    Independent Colleges and Universi-
    ties (NAICU)
NASFAA. *See* National Association of
    Student Financial Aid Administra-
    tors (NASFAA)
NASULGC. *See* National Association of
    State Universities and Land-Grant
    Colleges (NASULGC)
National Association for Equal Opportu-
    nity in Higher Education (NAFEO),
    72
National Association of College and
    University Attorneys (NACUA), 71
National Association of College and
    University Business Officers
    (NACUBO), 71
National Association of Independent
    Colleges and Universities (NAICU),
    72
National Association of State Universities
    and Land-Grant Colleges
    (NASULGC), 72

National Association of Student Financial
    Aid Administrators (NASFAA), 72
National Council of University Research
    Administrators (NCURA), 72
National Education Association (NEA),
    72
National Endowment for the Arts (NEA)
    forms, 86-96
    news releases from, 69
National Endowment for the Humanities
    (NEH)
    abstract for, 14
    directory of, 69-70
    forms, 97-103
    news releases from, 69
National Home Study Council, 72
National Institutes of Health (NIH)
    news releases from, 69
    shortcomings found in proposals,
        28-29
National Science Foundation (NSF)
    forms, 104-07
    news releases from, 69
National University of Continuing
    Education Association (NUCEA), 72
Naumann, St. Elmo, 6
NCURA. *See* National Council of
    University Research Administrators
    (NCURA)
NEA. *See* National Education Association
    (NEA); National Endowment for the
    Arts (NEA)
NEH. *See* National Endowment for the
    Humanities (NEH)
News, Notes and Deadlines, 69, 133
News releases, 69
NIH. *See* National Institutes of Health
    (NIH)
NIH Guide for Grants and Contracts, 69,
    133
Nonprofit institutions
    feedback relation between ideas
        and, 3-4
    Internal Revenue Service
        definition of, 4-5
    method for helping ideas to serve,
        4
    people involved in the develop-
        ment of ideas, 7-9
    role and responbility of, 6
NSF. *See* National Science Foundation
    (NSF)
NSF Bulletin, 69, 133
NUCEA. *See* National University of
    Continuing Education Association
    (NUCEA)

Objectives, 15
Originator of idea
    finding a source for support, 30-
        31
    role and resopnsibilities of, 6-8

Personnel
    involved in development of ideas,
      7-9
    section in proposal, 18-19
Philanthropic Digest, 133
President/Chancellor, 8
Problem statement, 14
Procedures, section of grant proposal, 15
Project Director, 7-8, 36
Proposal. *See* Grant proposal
Protection of Human Subjects Assurance,
    121

Public Health Service Grants, 133
Review process for proposals, 21-29

Sample forms. *See* Forms
Schedule. *See* Activity schedule/status
    report
"Selected U.S. Government Publica-
    tions," 70
Smithsonian Institution, 69
Status report. *See* Activity schedule/status
    report
Summative evaluation, 21

Table of contents, 13
Telephone books, 69-70
Timetable, for idea development, 9, 10
Transmittal letter, 33
Typing requirements, 33-34

USDA. *See* Department of Agriculture

Washington International Arts Letter, 133
Wessell, Nils Y., 31